The elements of seamanship

Second Edition

The elements
of seamanship

THE SEAMANSHIP SERIES

Roger C. Taylor

drawings by Jim Sollers

INTERNATIONAL MARINE
PUBLISHING COMPANY
Camden, Maine 04843

This book is dedicated to
Dave Cabot
with whom I had great fun
practicing the elements of seamanship

Published by International Marine Publishing Company

Library of Congress Cataloging in Publication Data

Taylor, Roger C.
  The elements of seamanship.

  Includes index.
  1. Seamanship.   I. Title
GV777.5.T39   1986   623.88   86-113
ISBN 0-87742-220-6

Questions regarding the content of this book should be
addressed to:

International Marine Publishing Company
Division of TAB Books, Inc.
P.O. Box 220
Camden, Maine 04843

Contents

Preface

What I have tried to do in this book is envision myself going on the water at my careful best and remember to tell you as many as possible of the things going through my head. I've tried to keep to basics and not give you a lot of detail except where I thought it really important to do so. I've tried to keep the book short. Yet I haven't been able to resist tossing in a sea story here and there when I thought of one to illustrate a point or catch you dozing off.

The result is a book that is much more about the art of seamanship than about its science. I hope you'll find my book useful on the water—my aim has been to produce something practical—but you'll still need books of the facts of seamanship to tell you in detail about the construction and performance of a specific pump, the latest changes to the Rules of the Road, preventive maintenance routines on your marine engine, the breaking strength of various sizes of chain, or the legal requirements for lifesaving devices on board your vessel. Fortunately, there are plenty of good books that can tell you all these kinds of facts.

And now let me just say that should you spy my vessel on the water, do not expect her to be handled by a faultless seaman. I've misjudged every situation in this book at least twice and probably will again. Writing it all down doesn't make me any more immune from making mistakes than reading it does you. See you out there.

Roger C. Taylor
Camden, Maine

1

Keeping the Water Out

One object there is still which I never pass without the renewed wonder of childhood, and that is the bow of a boat. . . . It is a simple work, but it will keep out water.

John Ruskin

A vessel may be defined as an object that keeps water either in or out; it is the latter sort that concerns us.

Keeping the water out is not only the first and most important element of seamanship, but also it is the only necessary element of seamanship. All the other elements of seamanship are niceties, but keeping the water out is a necessity. Whatever else may befall your vessel, if you can keep the water out of her (and hang onto her), you won't drown.

Going on the water without drowning is the sure proof of successful seamanship. Drowning may be proof that seamanship failed, but there is no denying that the sea can

"Keeping the water out is not only the first and most important element of seamanship, but also it is the only necessary element of seamanship. All the other elements of seamanship are niceties, but keeping the water out is a necessity." Photo by Norm Holm. Courtesy, National Fisherman.

call into play elemental forces of such ferocity that no skill of seamanship can save the sailor.

I make no attempt here to discuss the vital element of luck, but I hereby acknowledge its omnipresence and its power to drown good seamen and save lousy ones.

I would like to announce at this time that the elements of seamanship are equally useful to both of the sexes, despite the masculinity of the word itself and my own continual use of masculine pronouns when referring to sailors.

The very first thing to do without fail every time you go on board any vessel, whether she belongs to you or to a stranger, is to look in the bilge down inside the bottom of the boat to see if there is any water in there. Don't ever assume a dry bilge. Look in there and see for yourself. (On a stranger's vessel, looking in the bilge may require tact or even secrecy, but do not be deterred.)

It's obviously helpful to divide up a vessel into watertight compartments. One of the most comforting things I had in my 25-foot schooner was a watertight bulkhead right across her middle.

Good seamanship requires a vivid imagination. The best of intentions and care cannot always ensure a dry bilge. Imagine your vessel half-full of water, and imagine how you will get it out. The quicker you can get the water out of your vessel, the better. More may be coming in even as you start.

GETTING THE WATER OUT

The best tool for removing water from a vessel is a bucket. Don't skimp on size, strength, or number. If access both to the water in the vessel and to her rail is available to more than one person, then more than one bucket may be used at once. Of course the distance from water to rail may require a bucket brigade, but I would hate to be a member of that brigade who had to wait precious seconds between bucket passes simply because there weren't enough buckets on board.

The horse people are way ahead of us sailors when it comes to buckets. Their black, somewhat flexible, heavy rubber ones are relatively light and easy to handle, yet seem indestructible. The lip of a flexible bucket can take the shape—somewhat—of that part of the vessel it is bailing. Metal buckets are all right. Plastic buckets may break, especially when it's cold. I'd hate to be scared, cold, and bailing like anything, only to have the bucket break.

3

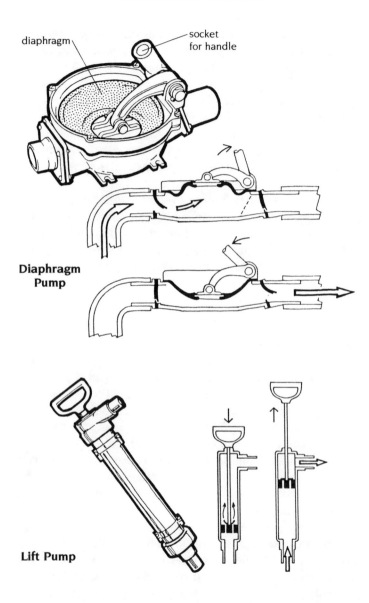

diaphragm

socket
for handle

**Diaphragm
Pump**

Lift Pump

*"Big diaphragm pumps and big lift pumps can move water fairly quickly.
Small pumps will move water slowly. Have big pumps, not small ones."*

Pumps can remove water from vessels. Big diaphragm pumps and big lift pumps can move water fairly quickly. Small pumps will move water slowly. Have big pumps, not small ones.

With suitable lengths of intake and discharge hoses on a pump, one person can move water all the way overboard from rather inaccessible places. But remember that if there is enough water inside the vessel to endanger her, most of it will probably be accessible to the bucket.

There are pumps that run on gasoline and pumps that run on electricity, as well as those that run on elbow grease. If the former are big pumps, they may be able to move water faster than can a seaman-operated pump. The seaman-operated pump will nearly always start and, within reason, run as long as needed. Portable pumps are more versatile and repairable than fixed pumps.

Bailers smaller than buckets can be bought, made, or improvised. The first bailer I had was a little rectangular bicarbonate of soda can (without the top) that exactly fit the rectangular bilge of my punt.

For drying out the bilge after bailing or pumping, nothing comes anywhere near an old towel. Never buy a sponge.

If the water gains on bailing and/or pumping, the only way to keep from sinking is to support the vessel other than by her own buoyancy. Think about borrowing buoyancy from one or more other vessels that may have a reserve of it to lend you. Tricky business, this, and fraught with potential danger to rescuer and rescued. Many strong lines, well attached, and many fenders would be the chief ingredients for success. If more than one of the adjacent vessels were rigged, you would have to focus part of your attention aloft. Collision would only complicate matters.

Think of supporting your vessel with a shoal bottom under her keel. In other words, think of running her ashore as a lesser evil than sinking. Here is a nice dilemma: How much crew energy do you devote to getting the water out and how much to propelling the vessel toward the shore? The idea, of course, is to get there before you sink.

If it's obvious you will get there before you sink, then you have some little choice about exactly what part of the shore you will use for your support. Look primarily for shelter from waves (both existing and future) and secondarily for evenness and softness of bottom.

I once had to run a 10-foot skiff ashore because she was gradually being overwhelmed by wind and sea, and I had no one to bail. Luckily (remember that ever-present factor?), there was to leeward a large sand flat covered with weeds. Their fronds welcomed and encircled us, keeping the waves away while I bailed the water out.

LEAKS AND THROUGH-HULL VALVES

Even though your vessel has been designed and built specifically to keep water out, still there are many ways for it to get in, some obvious, some insidious.

If the material from which the hull of a vessel is made is in more than one piece, the joint or joints may leak. Seams between wooden planks or the hull-to-deck joint on a fiberglass boat are obvious candidates. Leaks in a joint occur because the joint opens up for some reason. Adjacent fastenings may carry away. The stuff that was crammed into it to make it watertight may come adrift. These calamities are generally caused, in turn, by sudden stress on the hull, either by the hull's hitting something, such as a wave, the bottom, or another hull, or by severe stress being imparted to the hull by the rig through carrying too much sail when it's blowing hard.

Pay close attention to your hull joints, and do everything in your power to make them strong and watertight before you put your vessel in the water. Having done that, take the precaution of doing everything in your power to keep your vessel from hitting anything, and don't put undue stress on your rig and thus on your hull.

Some designers and builders drill holes right through

the hulls of vessels below the waterline. The truth is that some sailors, myself included at times, give a higher priority to such mundane activities as cooling their engines, pumping their water closets, and draining their sinks than they do to keeping the water out of their vessels. Perhaps they think they can do both at once. If you yourself are tempted to try these tricks, remember that it is a dangerous business to drill holes in something that is supposed to keep water out. Take precautions.

If, for example, you have a hole in the hull of your vessel for the pipe that drains the sink, have the pipe as strong as the hull, because you are now depending on the pipe as much as on the hull to keep the water out of your vessel. Have a valve in the pipe just as close to the hull as you can. You can use the valve to shut the sea out of the pipe if the pipe should fail for any reason. Of course the valve must be as strong as the hull. It should also be the simplest type of valve so as little as possible can go wrong with it. The simplest type of valve is the gate valve, the kind that slides a heavy gate across the opening in the pipe as you turn the handle clockwise. (When you open a valve and leave it open, don't leave it jammed open, for you may not be able to shut it again just when you want to most. Open it all the way, and then give the handle one-eighth of a turn toward shut. That way the valve is always ready to be shut quickly.)

Don't cover holes through your hull with built-in furniture. Be able to reach those holes. Cut a tapered wooden plug to fit every hole in your hull, and keep the plugs handy.

There once was a lad who had a hole in his boat into which water was pouring. He sought advice about this and was told to bore another hole in his boat so that the water could run back out. This he did. The boat sank, and the boy drowned. When I first heard this story, I thought it wasn't true, but years later, in a 44-foot yawl, I found that it was true. We went on board and looked in the bilge. There was a lot of water in there, and it was gradually getting deeper.

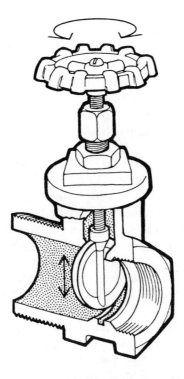

"The simplest type of valve is the gate valve, the kind that slides a heavy gate across the opening in the pipe as you turn the handle clockwise."

The vessel had a permanently installed bilge pump to remove any water that might get into her either through any of several underwater holes that had been drilled in her hull or by any other route. But someone had advised the builder of the vessel that it would be a good idea to drill still another underwater hole in the hull out through which the pump could discharge water. The check valve in the pump was broken, and it was through this last hole that water was pouring in.

If a vessel has one or more engines, she will have to have one or more propeller shafts going out through holes in the hull to connect the engines with propellers. Here is

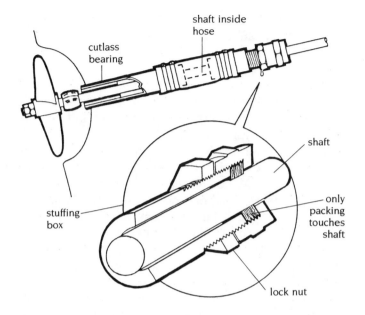

cutlass bearing

shaft inside hose

shaft

stuffing box

only packing touches shaft

lock nut

"If you leave the shaft bearing loose enough so that the shaft will turn with the greatest of ease, water will leak in around the shaft; if you tighten the stuffing box around the shaft bearing so tight that no water can leak in, the shaft won't turn. So you compromise and get a drip."

another nice dilemma: If you leave the shaft bearing loose enough so that the shaft will turn with the greatest of ease, water will leak in around the shaft; if you tighten the stuffing box around the shaft bearing so tight that no water can leak in, the shaft won't turn. So you compromise and get a drip. That's all right, but a stuffing box changes. A turning shaft wears away packing. When a vessel is out of water, packing dries out. Be suspicious of stuffing boxes.

When a friend and I went on board a handsome sloop to fetch her home from the yard, the first thing we did was look in the bilge. There was a lot of water in there. It happened to be coming in through the stuffing box, which needed tightening. No big thing, but we were glad to have discovered this little problem before getting underway.

Watertight cockpits are only as watertight as their way of draining their water back overboard. Cockpit drains and their through-hull valves must all be as strong as the hull.

As if it were not enough that the sea has so many methods of finding its way into your vessel, the very heavens themselves occasionally open up and rain down into your vessel from overhead. There is nothing deceptive about this way Mother Nature has of trying to sink you, and only in extreme cases of procrastination at the pump will she succeed. Of course sailors whose vessels have watertight decks, hatches, and cockpits may laugh at the rain. It is only those sailors whose bilges are directly or indirectly open to the sky who need worry.

Unwanted liquid in your bilge may not always come from sea or sky. Freshwater tanks have been known to spring leaks, as have fuel tanks. But here we are talking about the mere untidiness of having a certain type of liquid come unstowed; there is no danger of sinking. In such an event, the automatic electric bilge pump can play a nasty trick on you. As fast as your diesel fuel leaks into the bilge, this helpful little fellow chucks it right overboard without so much as a by-your-leave. This happened to me in the Bay of Fundy one night, and I had twelve hours of a slatting calm in which to lecture myself about being unobservant.

WIND AND WAVE

The chief reason I like to go on the water is that I am endlessly fascinated by its waves. Perpetual motion. These beguiling waves, however, can make it very hard for a sailor to keep water out of his vessel. They may become large and steep and break right over the top of the vessel, or they may become even larger and steeper and catch the vessel up in their crests as they break, flinging her down on her beam ends, or, worse, turning her upside down.

Waves are caused mostly by the wind. And the wind, by

itself, can cause water to get into a vessel, at least a sailing vessel, by heeling her over so far that openings into the top of the vessel are submerged. The sailor's most common complaint of this nature is when the gunwale of his small, open boat goes under.

It is prudent for the seaman to study these phenomena of wave and wind while he can, from the security of dry land, and use his vivid imagination to envision how he would cope with their various sizes and strengths.

Wind

Let's imagine the wind first. Study the Beaufort Scale (page 100) carefully. Note the descriptions of the sea for each wind force; think about the descriptions of how traditional vessels react to each. Imagine how your vessel would react under various sail combinations to each force of wind described.

A vessel will generally "take" more wind than you think she will. Still, lack of respect for the strength of the wind could earn you an obituary similar to this one printed in an 18th-century English newspaper: "By obstinately carrying too much sail he ran the boat under water."

The worst trick the wind can play on you is suddenly to blow two or three times as hard as it has been blowing and, if it really wants to be nasty, blow all at once from abeam instead of from on the bow. Your vessel will be knocked down. Any opening that goes under will admit a torrent of water.

To prevent a knockdown, start by watching the water to windward ("keep a weather eye open"), so you'll be forewarned of a gust. When a hard gust strikes, the first thing to do is luff. Ease the boat up into the wind a ways, just a little if the gust is not too hard, and quite a lot if it is very hard. The idea is to ease her just enough to keep the water out and no more. If you ease her more than enough to keep the water out, you'll lose speed to no purpose.

"The idea is to ease her just enough to keep the water out and no more. If you ease her more than enough to keep the water out, you'll lose speed to no purpose." Photo by Chris Cunningham. Courtesy, Sail magazine.

In any event, you don't want to luff her so much that she loses steerageway. A boat that is caught in a gust and won't answer her helm is vulnerable to a severe knockdown, precisely because she *can't* be luffed.

If luffing won't keep the water out, ease your sheets, too. Don't belay the sheet—that is, make it fast to a cleat—in a little boat. Unless the boat has a lot of weather helm, it's important to ease the jib sheet as well as the main sheet. If you ease the main sheet only, she may pay off just when you want her to luff.

If the blast is of such ferocity that luffing and easing

sheets still won't keep the water out, then you need to let go halyards, get the sails down, and take stock of the situation.

One time a big gang of us were out sailing my 37-foot skipjack on Chesapeake Bay. A fresh northeaster backed to northwest and suddenly breezed right up. We were already scalding back for Annapolis and didn't realize the northwester really meant business until, with the wind about abeam, we received a blast that sent the lee bulwarks under and allowed water to come thundering up across a wide, flat deck that was tilted to an angle we'd never seen before. Such violence seemed to call for a drastic reaction. Skipping mere luffing and easing of sheets, I ran from wheel to mast, threw off the main halyard, and hauled down hard on its other end. (I used to tie the bitter end of the main halyard into the head of the sail with a bowline so it went aloft with the sail as it was hoisted and could be used later for a downhaul.) In a very short time, we were racing happily along under just the jib with the hauled-down mainsail held up on the well-eased boom by its many lazyjacks. There was little in that rig capable—by failing or jamming—of preventing one person from reducing the vessel's sail area by 600 square feet in a few seconds.

In a little vessel the unexpected shifting of live ballast can cause water to get in. Once a friend and I were trying out an uncle's new little plywood catboat. We were running up the river dead before a fresh breeze. It came time to jibe, and as we prepared for the maneuver, unbeknown to me, my friend was reasoning to himself that if the crew changed sides when tacking, then he must also change sides when jibing. When we jibed, he came over to my side of the boat along with the boom. That's the only time in my life I ever tipped a boat over.

Keep your weight low in a small boat, using it to help, rather than harm, stability.

Don't try to outguess thunder squalls. Assume every one of them is going to blow a living gale for a short time.

You can be overpowered by a breeze that is consistently

too much for your vessel even under much-reduced sail. That's what led to my running my little sailing skiff into protective weeds on a lee shore. We were crossing a fairly wide river, and she was half-full of water with two-thirds of the way to go. In that situation, I thought tacking and broad reaching back was less likely to result in a capsize than stopping and bailing out, even with the sail down. I thought my best chance to keep her from taking in any more water was to get her moving toward shelter, under sail but not close-hauled.

Some people say you should practice capsizing "so you won't be afraid of it." I say you *should* be afraid of tipping over, especially if the water is at all cold, and that you should practice assiduously at *not* capsizing.

If your vessel is decked over and well ballasted, you can drive her in a breeze without much danger of water getting in as long as your deck openings are strong and tightly sealed. But it is far better to reduce sail and take it easy on boat and crew.

Wave

While strong winds can lead indirectly to water entering your vessel, there is just nothing like a big wave for undoing directly and suddenly all your efforts at keeping the water out.

Observe waves on all scales from mud puddle ripples to great ocean breakers. Watch how small waves combine and how a wave runs in—unexpectedly—from a new direction. When big seas do this, they are at their most dangerous.

Imagine your vessel's response to every wave you see. Realize that wind strength is only one factor in wave making; fetch and the length of time the wind has been blowing are equally important. An oceanographer named Charles Bretschneider did a great service to sailors by writing equations (later portrayed in a graph, see page 101) showing the interrelationship of the three factors and their effect on wave size.

The first indication you get that waves want to deposit part of their contents inside your vessel is spray. When water, even in small quantities, o'erleaps the rail, there is more to follow unless something changes. The hope in a sailor's heart often convinces him that the waves will get smaller so the spray will stop flying. Such optimism may or may not prove to be well founded, but when the spray begins to fly, you should start thinking about either slowing down your vessel or changing her course to go more with the waves. Few sailors mind a little spray flying. The tang of salt on the lips. Invigorating. Also a warning that the waves are trying to get into your vessel.

The thing to be avoided is shipping a sea. A sea contains a very large amount of water, and some or all of it coming on board may find its way inside, depending on whether your vessel is open or decked and whether or not her deck openings are sealed. A great deal of water traveling along at some speed represents a great deal of force, and this force may do damage to your vessel. The same people who groan under the weight of a ten-gallon jerry can of water pretend to be surprised when big, fast-moving seas bend heavy steel stanchions.

You can avoid shipping a head sea by steering carefully and by slowing down your vessel. It's amazing how much small differences in speed make in a head sea.

You can avoid shipping a sea over the side of your vessel by steering carefully, by running off more with the seas, or by heaving-to with the sea on the bow. Don't forget when sailing a small open boat that a powerboat going by to leeward will send a beam sea right toward your perhaps nearly submerged lee gunwale. When this happens to me, I let the sheet run just before the guy's waves hit me, so that the nearly submerged gunwale will come right up to its normal height with the boat level. Then, as soon as the waves go by, I trim in again smartly and resume sailing as before I was so rudely interrupted.

To avoid shipping a sea over the stern of your vessel—getting pooped, they call it—you can steer carefully or round up and heave-to, taking the sea on the bow. Some sailors say slowing down helps when running in a big seaway, while others say speeding up helps. The former theory is based on creating a wake that is less turbulent and so less likely to cause a following sea to break on board. The latter theory is based on reducing the relative speed of the overtaking sea and on being able to maneuver away from breaking crests. The fact remains that as long as you keep a big breaking sea astern, there is always danger of getting pooped. Depending on circumstances, it may be more or less of a danger than shipping a sea when hove-to with the waves on the bow, or shipping a sea with the vessel lying ahull (simply left to her own devices with no sail set and the sea coming from somewhere near the weather beam).

Whichever way you head your vessel in big breaking seas, it may be possible to get some measure of protection from a long loop of anchor line let out to windward and/or the casting of oil upon the waters. A most promising tactic to me is lying ahull with a big loop of line up to windward, adjusted at the ends of the vessel to keep the sea abaft the beam, and with oil spread inside the bight.

Whatever tactics you use in heavy weather, you'll be thankful if your vessel has enough ballast, fairly deep in the water and securely attached to the vessel, to give her good stability. Though shipping a sea is certainly to be avoided, it need not be a disaster if your vessel is decked, has a watertight cockpit, and has her deck openings strongly sealed. It's a good idea to have deck openings as near the centerline as possible. The more deck openings, the harder to keep the water out.

SURVIVAL

The worst thing the sea can do is turn your vessel upside down. A wave may roll her right down on her beam ends

"The worst thing the sea can do is turn your vessel upside down. A wave may roll her right down on her beam ends and on over." U.S. Coast Guard photo. Courtesy, National Fisherman.

and on over. Or one may lift her stern so high that her bow digs in, she trips, and does a somersault—with a half-twist thrown in or not, as the case may be. "Pitch poling" is the all-too-descriptive term used.

Imagining these horrors, sailors begin to think of very strong companionway hatchboards that are locked *down* into position, coupled with very strong companionway slides locked *aft*. They think of hatches, skylights, and lids to those abominable cockpit lockers that ought to be outlawed because they are not lockers at all but rather great caverns that open the whole after part of the vessel to

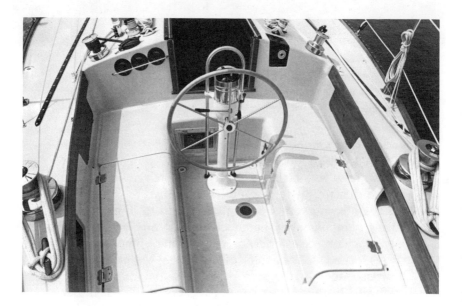

Above: "Or one may lift her stern so high that her bow digs in, she trips, and does a somersault—with a half-twist thrown in or not, as the case may be. 'Pitch poling' is the all-too-descriptive term used." **Below:** "Imagining these horrors, sailors begin to think of lids to cockpit lockers that can be dogged shut at each corner against a heavy gasket." Courtesy, Sail magazine.

the cockpit—hatches, skylights, and lids that can be dogged shut at each corner against a heavy gasket. They think of heavy shutters that can be dogged down over cabin-house windows. (The danger is not always the direct assault of the wave coming down on you from the weather side. The *Vertue* XXXV, a small, seagoing cutter, had her *lee* deckhouse window smashed in by a sea when a wave rolled her down against that sea.)

If you want to read a hair-raising story of people keeping enough water out of a vessel rolled over by huge seas to keep her afloat and get her going again, read Miles Smeeton's account of how he and his wife, Beryl, and their companion, John Guzzwell, did just that in their ketch *Tzu Hang* in the Roaring Forties. The book is called *Once is Enough*.

Shipping a sea in an open boat, a half-decked boat, or a boat with an open cockpit is something else again. It is A Very Good Thing, of course, if such vessels can remain afloat even though full of water. An unballasted, wooden boat can, but a ballasted boat or any boat made of a dense hull material will need flotation, in the form of light plastic material, or air tanks, or maybe even inflatable air bags, if she is to stay afloat when full of water.

A good sailor realizes that however clever his tactics for keeping waves out of his vessel, there can come along someday a wave big and steep enough to destroy all his defenses, get inside his vessel, and fill her right up. A good sailor can imagine that happening to him.

As long as your vessel stays afloat, stay with her. Your greatest chance of saving your life is to save your vessel. When that proves impossible, and your vessel founders, then you need a life raft or dinghy to climb into. That gives you another tiny vessel out of which to try to keep the water. If you don't have such a vessel, you ought at least to have something that will float for a long time.

In such an extreme situation, your worst enemy will be despair. The best antidote to despair is mental preparation, or imagining-it-happening. Reading the stories of survivors can help. The best one I know of is *The Bombard Story* by Alain Bombard.

The most important element of seamanship is keeping the water out of your vessel. The other elements of seamanship pale into relative insignificance when compared with keeping the water out. Still, there *is* more to seamanship than staying dry. In the next chapter, we'll talk about keeping from hitting anything.

2

Keeping From Hitting Anything

A *collision at sea can ruin your entire day.*

Thucydides

The second most important element of seamanship is keeping from hitting anything. Depending usually upon whether the thing you hit is at sea or in harbor, collisions are at most dangerous and at least embarrassing. A collision may be between your vessel and other man-made structures, such as another vessel, a buoy, or a dock, or it may be between your vessel and the bottom. The latter type may be a grounding, a stranding, or a shipwreck, depending on the length of time your vessel stays on the bottom.

If you would keep your vessel from hitting anything, watch. "Watch" is an ancient marine word. A phrase such as

"The most important place to watch is the water ahead, through which—after all—your vessel is about to go." Photo by W.H. Ballard. Courtesy, National Fisherman.

"Relieve the watch!" echoes down the centuries of seafaring. At sea, the very day is divided into "watches."

According to my dictionary, "watch" means "to look or observe attentively or carefully; be closely observant."

From an early age, the child is told, "Watch where you're going!" Good advice. The most important place to watch is the water ahead, through which—after all—your vessel is about to go. It is important to notice if that particular patch of water happens to have in it another vessel, a funny-looking dark shadow with a swirl of waves round it, or a large baulk of timber.

Rowing is a special case, because you're facing the wrong way to watch where you're going. Don't be ashamed to keep on looking over your shoulder.

Once I was officer of the deck in a destroyer proceeding up the Mississippi River to New Orleans. The ship was being conned by the river pilot we had picked up inside the Delta. We went right on up at twenty knots. The pilot was an amiable fellow who could and did tell a story about nearly every bayou we passed. What impressed me was that all the time he kept chattering away, he never seemed to stop staring ahead at the River.

Do not concentrate your attention ahead to the exclusion of the rest of the horizon. When the submarine in which I spent a couple of years of my youth was submerged at periscope depth, every little while we would "Up scope for a look around." This was a rapid but methodical sweep through 360 degrees to see who might be sneaking up on us. It's an excellent procedure in a surface vessel.

Have as few obstructions to vision as possible on your vessel. Have high steering positions and low deckhouses. Do not blind yourself with low-cut headsails. Do not expect you can sail around with a deck-sweeping genoa jib set without hitting anything, unless you station a continuous bow watch.

If you have the luxury of a wheelhouse, don't stand your whole watch in it. Keep going outside for a better look, especially at night or in fog.

Use binoculars. Remember that they gather light to your eyes at night. To pick up dim objects on the horizon at night, look a little above or below the horizon to present them to the most light-sensitive parts of your eyes.

At Navy schools, you have to memorize a lot of stuff. One statement that has been parroted back a few million times is: "Eternal vigilance is the price of safety."

The Rules of the Road specify that a vessel shall keep "a proper lookout." Courts have interpreted a proper lookout

"Do not blind yourself with low-cut headsails. Do not expect you can sail around with a deck-sweeping genoa jib set without hitting anything, unless you station a continuous bow watch." Photo Revue Neptune. Courtesy, Sail magazine.

to mean a trained, vigilant seaman, properly stationed, and with no duty assigned other than looking out. Because of the latter requirement, helmsmen have been held by the courts not to be proper lookouts. Of course it is not practical for shorthanded small craft always to station a proper lookout. By definition, the singlehander is nearly always in violation of the court's interpretation of the Rule. Such violation is only a concern if you hit something. To keep from hitting anything, the helmsman and every other person on deck should be, insofar as possible, acting as a lookout.

COLLISION

The first consideration in keeping from hitting another vessel is to determine when risk of collision exists. Risk of collision exists when another vessel is closing with your

"The best way to take a bearing on another vessel is with a pelorus mounted on your compass." Photo by Eric Hiscock. Courtesy, Sail magazine.

vessel on a steady compass bearing. Take a bearing on the other vessel early, while he is still some distance away. (When referring to other vessels you are trying to keep from hitting, refer to them as he, not she. That vessel you are trying to keep from hitting is controlled by a person,* and what you are trying to do is read that person's mind. For example, when the other vessel makes an unexpected turn toward you, you might utter, "What the hell's he trying to do now?")

The Rules of the Road state: "If the bearing does not appreciably change, such risk |of collision| should be deemed to exist." Quaint. Deem, hell, it damned well *does* exist.

The best way to take a bearing on another vessel is with a pelorus mounted on your compass. If you don't have such

---

There was an announcement in Chapter 1 about the elements of seamanship applying equally to both of the sexes.

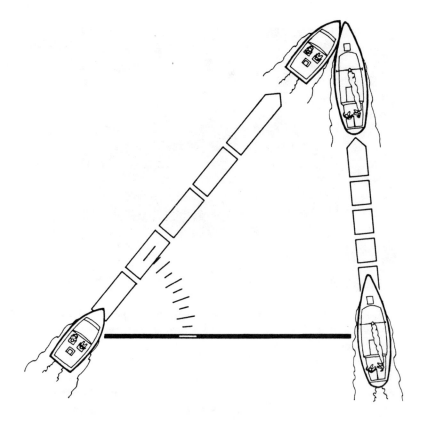

"Observe whether his angle on the bow is steady or changing. If the aspect of his vessel as you look at her remains constant, the bearing is steady." (In this example, his angle on the bow is starboard 50 degrees, and it stays constant. So his bearing stays steady at West. So you ruin each other's day.)

sophisticated gear, use a hand-bearing compass. If you don't have one of those, use your extended hand for a pelorus on your compass. If you don't have a compass, observe whether or not you are making land on him. Is he slowly moving along the land in sight behind him? If not, the bearing is steady. If there is no land in sight behind him, observe whether his angle on the bow (that's what it's called, but it's actually *your* angle on *his* bow)* is steady or changing. If the aspect of his vessel as you look at her remains constant, the bearing is steady.

Remember that when two vessels are closing with each other, their relative speed will be the sum of their speed vectors.

If you are to keep from hitting another vessel that is closing with your vessel on a steady bearing, you must change course and/or speed. He may change course and/ or speed, but then again, he may not. You can depend upon your own actions; you can't depend on his.

In submarine school, it was explained to us that because submarines have so little reserve buoyancy, they usually sink when they hit another vessel. We were urged not to let that happen. The method prescribed was defensive maneuvering. We were told to take avoiding action early.

One of the best defensive maneuvers is to stop. Take all way off your vessel. Another good defensive maneuver is to make a huge circle away from the other vessel and then come back on your course and keep going as if he had never been there.

There may not always be enough space to maneuver well clear of another vessel. Geography, the presence of other vessels, or mere convenience may require that you allow your vessel to come close enough to another so that the only way to keep from hitting him is for the two of you to do a careful dance past each other according to elaborate, rigid choreography. The various dance steps are prescribed in the Rules of the Road.

Get a good book on the Rules of the Road and learn the

---

* Angle on the bow is a fancy way of measuring the aspect of a vessel as you look at her. It's the angle your bearing from the vessel makes with the vessel, measured from his bow either port or starboard through 180 degrees. So if you bear dead ahead of him, you're looking right at his bow, and the angle on the bow is zero. If you're looking at his port beam, the angle on the bow is port 90; if at his starboard bow, the angle on the bow is starboard 45, and so forth.

Steering and Sailing Rules—in particular—cold. The best book on the Rules of the Road is *Farwell's Rules of the Nautical Road*, revised by Commander Frank E. Bassett, U.S. Navy, and Commander Richard A. Smith, Royal Navy. The book is published by the U.S. Naval Institute at Annapolis, Maryland, and is currently in its sixth (1982) edition. Read the court cases collected by Captain Raymond F. Farwell and Commanders Bassett and Smith.

Read the Rules of the Road. Comply.

When trying to keep from hitting another vessel while maneuvering under the Rules of the Road, make big, obvious course changes, not little, imperceptible ones.

The Rules tell you which vessel, in various maneuvering situations, is privileged to "stand on" and which vessel is burdened to "give way" by changing course and/or speed. Of course when the situation becomes tight, it is no privilege to have to stand on, and no burden to have to give way.

The three basic maneuvering situations are: meeting, crossing, and overtaking.

When meeting, never turn left. Don't come left even the tiniest bit. If it looks as if you are going to pass the other vessel starboard-to-starboard, and you are uncomfortable about the closeness of the approach, make a great big, early right turn, so you can then come back on course and pass comfortably far away, port-to-port.

When crossing with another vessel, never turn left. If you're on the right, you must stand on. If you're on the left, you must give way. Turn right and/or slow down to let the other vessel cross ahead. Don't try to cross ahead of a vessel that must stand on, unless you will cross well ahead.

When overtaking another vessel, keep well way from him. Remember that a sailing vessel overtaking a power-driven vessel must maneuver to keep clear of the latter.

The Rules always give the right of way to the less maneuverable vessel. Never press your right of way. Always doubt the other vessel's intentions—"his" intentions—and be ready to maneuver defensively, no matter that you have the right of way through being on the starboard tack when he's on the port tack, or through being under sail when he's under power.

The Rules require that certain working vessels be given the right of way. If you are in a yacht, make it your rule to give every working vessel the right of way. He's earning his living.

Give boats under oars the right of way, unless they are overtaking.

Watch out for large vessels. They are nowhere near as maneuverable as your small one. One of the hardest things for sailors of small craft to estimate, simply through lack of experience, is the course and speed of large vessels, particularly at night. Every time you see a large vessel underway, observe closely her course and speed. Estimating course means estimating angle on the bow. The key to estimating angle on the bow is the alignment of a vessel's masts. When you see a ship during daylight, notice precisely how the distance between her masts changes as her angle on the bow changes. At night, at a distance, all you will see is the white masthead light and the white range light, one on each mast; colored side lights are invisible until you are closer. The after range light is always taller than the forward masthead light. Knowing how the distance between a vessel's masts changes as her angle on the bow changes, you will be able to judge her angle on the bow—and thus her course—just by observing the relative positions of her two bright, white lights.

The key to estimating a big ship's speed is to look at her wake. Remember that big vessels don't start making much in the way of waves until they are really traveling. A 400-foot tanker at eight knots looks nearly dead in the water.

Once when standing watch with the skipper of a motorsailer crossing the Gulf of Maine on a nice moonlit night, we came across a deep-laden tanker easing in toward Portland to pick up his pilot at daybreak. He was making no fuss at all as he slid along. The skipper thought we'd cross his bow easily, but I prevailed upon him to make a large defensive circle to the right, let him go on about his business, and then cross under his stern. This we did, and the skipper was a little surprised to find that the tanker was going about twice as fast as we were.

If your vessel is small, her running lights are not likely to be notably visible. Have a powerful, beamed light ready to flash momentarily at the other vessel's helm and then on your sails. A split-second flash right at him will get his attention without blinding him. I emphasize *split-second*. I'd rather be on the receiving end of a beam of light flashed into my eyes momentarily than hit anything.

Fog complicates greatly watching for things you might hit and keeping from hitting them. If ever it is important to watch carefully, it is important in fog. To keep from hitting something in thick fog, you must espy its loom immediately the visibility allows.

Dark objects show up best in gray fog. Spruce-covered granite islands or rockweed-covered rocks show up better than sand dunes. Tanbarked sails show up better in fog than do white sails. Yet white foam from a sea breaking over a submerged reef fortunately can show up quite dazzlingly in fog.

It is very hard to judge distance in the fog, so when you first see the loom of something coming out of the fog, it's hard to know whether it is something fairly close, or something small very close. I remember once when a big dragger loomed out of the fog so close aboard as to take my breath away. A few seconds later the dragger changed itself into a seagull sitting in the water right beside us.

Reduce your speed in fog. The old axiom is that you must be able to stop in less than half the distance of visibility, for obvious reasons.

Blow fog signals. Listen for the fog signals of other vessels. Remember that the sound of your power plant can easily drown out the sound of the other vessels' fog signals. The dilemma is that with the engine shut down, you can't maneuver. When those famous seamen, Bert and I, in the

Bluebird, were listening for the Bangor Packet, the line was:

"'Cut engine, Bert.' BOI, BOI, Boi, boi, Sawhahw, sawhahw . . . sawhahw. Bert cut engine."

Now they could hear the Bangor Packet all right, and even exchanged signals with her, but they couldn't get out of her way. The *Bluebird* was "smuck."

If you hear the fog signal of another vessel ahead of you, slow right down and proceed with extreme caution until you hear the fog signal of the other vessel astern of you.

Radar on your vessel is not a license to speed in the fog. Plot the positions of the nearest vessels on a maneuvering board and figure their closest points of approach (CPA) to your vessel. Maneuver to keep well away from other vessels in the fog.

In fog, it is dangerous to assume that just because you cannot see the tow line of a tug, he has no tow.

Display a radar reflector in the fog. It will help other vessels equipped with radar to keep from hitting you.

GROUNDINGS

In order to keep from hitting bottom with your vessel, keep track of where you are relative to nearby pieces of bottom too shoal for you to get over. If you are not sure exactly where you are relative to such rocks and shoals, play it safe by steering a course you know is safe, even though it involves extra distance.

Watch where you're going. Read the water ahead before you try to sail through it.

Take soundings. Use a sounding pole. Use a leadline. Use an electronic sounding device. Take soundings.

Charts are remarkable documents and great bargains. A chart contains a vast array of accurate information recorded at great pains by the U.S. Coast and Geodetic Survey, now called the National Ocean Survey. I remember being

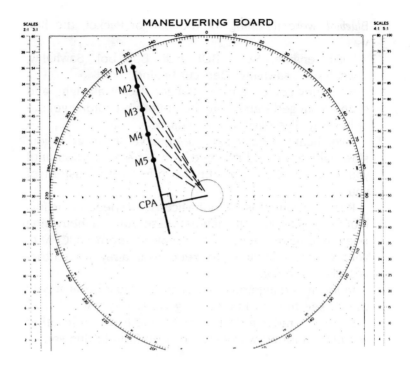

MANEUVERING BOARD

"Plot the positions of the nearest vessels on a maneuvering board and figure their closest points of approach to your vessel." (In the example, ranges and bearings M1 through M5 indicate a relative motion line that will produce a CPA bearing 260 at 3,000 yards.)

mightily impressed once when spending a day in one of their vessels, checking the accuracy of the chart of the mouth of the Severn River off Annapolis, impressed with the great amount of skill and detailed labor involved in merely verifying soundings. Every sounding you see printed on a chart is backed up by a lot more on huge worksheets.

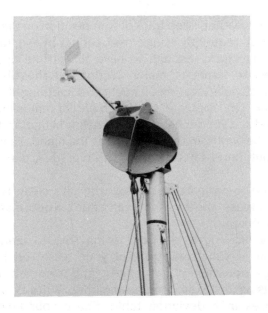

"Display a radar reflector in the fog. It will help other vessels equipped with radar to keep from hitting you." Courtesy, Sail magazine.

Don't skimp on charts. Buy them and use them. Don't be embarrassed to own a chart of your home waters and to consult it frequently. If you allow familiarity to breed contempt, you will probably hit something.

When sailing around in the vicinity of rocks and shoals, don't try to memorize the chart; keep consulting it.

Sailing with my father, I used to be amused that he couldn't read the soundings on the chart without his glasses. He could tell how many digits there were, though. He was particularly interested in the identification of any nearby single-digit numbers. He'd point at one and say, "What's that number?" And I'd be his eyes. It's not so funny now that I have to borrow my children's eyes for the same purpose. Sailing singlehanded is troublesome. I now have bifocals, so I can look from horizon to chart in a twinkling, no hands.

In good weather, keep track of your position on the chart roughly but frequently using cross bearings by eye; ranges, when you're lucky enough to have things line up; and distances in terms of major fractions of the distance between obvious locations. It might go something like this: "Let's see, I'm 'opposite' the south end of that island, its other end and yonder headland are nearly in line, and I'm a third of the way from that buoy to the mainland. That puts me about here. I'll tack well short of that unmarked ledge."

Prepare to navigate in the fog when it's clear. Have a good compass, the best you can afford. Keep magnetic stuff away from it.

Pick a nice quiet day and swing ship to learn the deviation of your compass. Put your vessel on known headings determined by ranges, and compare those headings against your compass heading. Write down the differences in a deviation table. Space your headings around the compass.

Learn to estimate the speed of your vessel accurately. Keep watching the bubbles go by and estimate her speed constantly. Check your estimates by measuring time and distance. The most important factor in fog navigation is knowing your course and speed accurately.

When sailing in clear weather in waters you frequent, notice the set of the current at different stages of the tide by watching a range over the stern or a changing point of fetch ahead on a steady compass course. It's nice to know what the current's doing to you when the fog shuts in. Whenever you pass any kind of buoy, observe the current flowing past it.

In fog, lay off your intended track ahead of time with courses and distances marked on the chart. As you proceed, write down the times at known points. Write down courses and speeds. Keep a good dead reckoning.

Fog comes and goes. A thick fog may clean out momentarily and then shut right down again. Take full advantage of any periods of greater visibility. Get any kind of fix you can, any time you can.

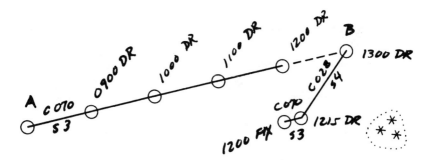

"Keep a good dead reckoning." (In this example, when the noon fix was plotted, it became apparent that to stand well clear of the rocks and get to point B at 1300, it was necessary to change course from 070 to 028 and increase speed from 3 knots to 4 knots.)

In fog, run for bold shores, places where you can stand in along a stretch of coastline with a good chance of seeing something before you hit it. Run for sound signals. Silent buoys are hard to find in the fog.

In the fog, listen for the rote. It's hard to judge the distance of the sound of breakers. Don't wait until you see their scary whiteness to change course.

A radio direction finder can help you find your way in fog. The easiest ones to operate, and thus the most accurate ones, are hand-held. Tricky stuff, RDF. The bearings are rough at best. Log everything you get. Keep at it continuously until you get the feel of the situation. Sometimes it is only when you have round after round of bearings that you begin to see which ones you can trust and which you can't. Loran can give you accurate positions in fog. Radar can reveal dangers unseen. All this electronics gear is worth having if you can afford it, but be prepared to fall back on a good dead reckoning and lively senses when the high-tech gear gets sick.

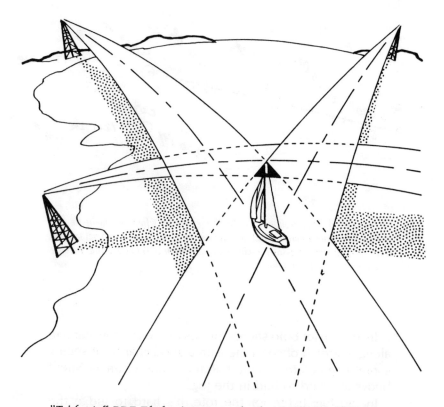

"Tricky stuff, RDF. The bearings are rough at best." (The most likely position is probably the little dark triangle, but don't put much faith in it. You could easily be in the bigger triangle formed by the dashed lines, or even in the huge triangle formed by the dotted lines and falling off the bottom of the drawing. Consult your log. Which of the three sets of bearings is most consistent? That's the dashed line to trust the most.)

At night, never take a navigational light for granted. Time it and time it until you are absolutely positive of its identification. Don't assume it's necessarily the light you expected it to be.

Use all possible navigational information. Develop the mentality of a Polynesian navigator. Observe all the elements of nature changing as you sail from one known position to another in clear weather. Don't forget to observe unnatural elements such as regular ferry and aircraft routes.

The best yarn I know about the creative use of navigational information was spun for me by Gil Hall, a Penobscot Bay pilot. Gil was bringing a vessel into Searsport under that most limited condition of visibility, heavy vapor or sea smoke, caused by extremely cold weather. He figured he was getting pretty close to the pier, but still couldn't see it and didn't dare keep creeping ahead. So he called down to the mate on the fo'c's'le head, "Throw something over." The mate understood, fetched an empty paint can, and sent it flying into the dense whiteness. It landed with a clank, not a splash. "I thought so," Gil muttered to himself and eased her on in alongside.

Sooner or later, sailing around in the fog, you'll get "lost." No matter. Trust what little information you have and proceed with caution. Take soundings. Try to fit them to the soundings on the chart. Even if they won't fit, there's nothing like a nice deep sounding to give you courage. You can always say to yourself, "I may be lost, but I ain't aground."

Be wary of running to a harbor to leeward in heavy weather. If you miss your way, you may have little recourse. If in doubt, stand off and wait for the weather to moderate.

Don't forget that with a big sea running, when you're in the trough, the depth over a shoal can be considerably less than shown on the chart.

When tacking to clear shoals in heavy weather, leave yourself room to try to tack, fail to get around, and have to fall back on the same tack, run off, jibe, and then head back up on the same tack.

Never put a sailing vessel in a spot where she is depending for her life on her engine.

I hate to run a boat aground even when there is no danger, like up a muddy creek. Never take running

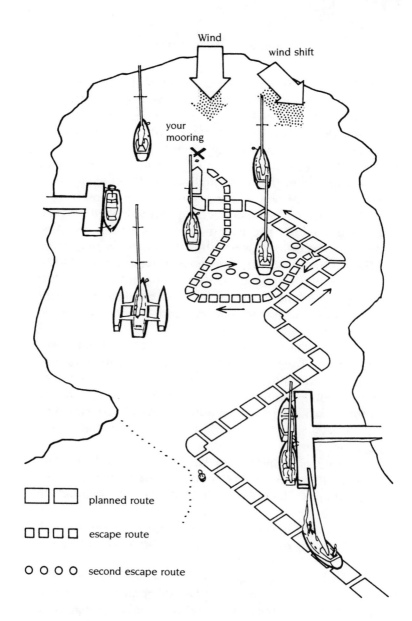

Wind

wind shift

your
mooring

planned route

escape route

second escape route

"Have an escape route planned in case you suddenly get headed and can't go where you want to after all." (The first escape route above is utilized in the event of a counterclockwise wind shift at a critical juncture. The second escape route is then planned in case the wind shifts clockwise again.)

aground casually. Remember that a centerboard can be a good sounding device. Keep that sounding pole handy, and don't be ashamed to use it frequently.

HARBOR WORK

Harbor collisions, though usually less dangerous than collisions at sea, are often more embarrassing. They are often well attended.

Watch out for the tide setting you into stationary harbor objects, such as moored boats, buoys, and the ends of docks. When sailing a small boat in a puffy breeze, and an obstruction close aboard to windward keeps you from luffing, be ready to slack the sheet right out in a puff. When maneuvering under sail in a light and fluky breeze, keep steerageway on your vessel at all costs. Have an escape route planned in case you suddenly get headed and can't go where you want to after all. Plenty of times working up into Camden's inner harbor in my little schooner, I used to end up sailing in circles before the breeze let me fetch through between the closely moored boats to my float.

If silent buoys are hard to find in the fog, unlighted ones seem all too easy to hit at night. Watch out for them. And when your vessel becomes a silent, anchored object at night, help to keep people from hitting her by setting a riding light.

When you bring your vessel into a dock, make an "eggshell" landing. This is the kind where you can hold an egg between your vessel and the dock as she comes in— without cracking the shell. Move in slowly.

When I told my friend Llewellyn Howland how much fun it was to make landings in the submarine across the tide of Connecticut's Thames River, he said correctly, "It's all a matter of judging pace and distance."

Play it safe. Move in for your landing with patience and slow grace. Land with majesty, not panic.

When landing under power, don't depend on a big backing bell; you may never get it.

The most spectacular landing I ever witnessed was that of a submarine in the hands of a Turkish crew to whom the vessel was in the process of being turned over. They brought her in fast, rang up All Back Full, and got—nothing. She marched right up along the dock to the head of her slip, her bow cut through 12 x 12s "protecting" the roadway as if they weren't there, and she tore into several feet of concrete, bursting miscellaneous steam and water pipes as she went—before finally grinding to a halt.

When coming in for a landing under sail, remember that a big, heavy boat will generally shoot a lot farther than you think she will, sometimes seemingly forever. We used to bring the 72-foot yawl *Royono* in for landings under sail. The trick was to be sure to get all the wind out of the mainsail long before you thought you needed to. Keep her just enough across the wind so that when you need that "slow ahead" bell, you can trim the main sheet in just a bit. If your vessel can be controlled with just her mainsail set, by all means simplify your landing by coming in under mainsail alone. Hold the sheet yourself, so there will be no misunderstanding about when to slack it. Remember that the main boom, shoved right out, will back the sail and give you a nice brake, but don't rely on this brake if you're really coming in too fast. When you misjudge the pace and distance, and are coming in too fast, make a big defensive circle and try again.

Always pick the lee side of the dock for a landing if you can. If you have to land on the weather side of the dock, get her stopped off a ways, and let the wind set you in on the dock slowly. If wind and tide are taking you away from the dock, get a line over and make it fast somewhere amidships. Then you can go ahead or astern on it as the case may be and use it to spring yourself right in alongside.

I suppose fenders have no place in a discussion of keeping from hitting anything, but don't be embarrassed

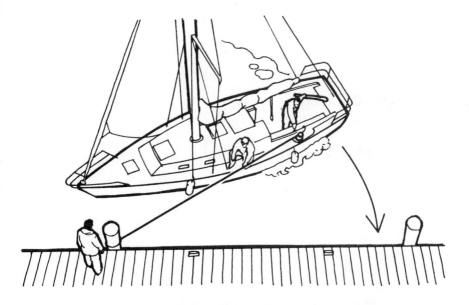

"If wind and tide are taking you away from the dock, get a line over and make it fast somewhere amidships. Then you can go astern on it and use it to spring yourself right in alongside."

to use them, anyway. The best kind are the big, round, red, plastic commercial fishing floats.

My simple message is: If you keep on watching where you're going, you probably will keep from hitting anything; if you don't, you won't.

Now, lest you despair that all the elements of seamanship are negative, let me say that the next chapter will discuss a positive element of seamanship: Keeping Her Going.

3

Keeping Her Going

Speed, bonnie boat, like a bird on the wing;
Onward, the sailors cry;. . . .

Skye Boat Song,
by Harold Edwin Boulton

The element of seamanship that is the most fun is keeping her going. Try to let your boat do her best all the time. Don't drive her unmercifully, but do give her every reasonable chance to show what she can do.

TRIM

If you would make a boat go, pay close attention to her trim. The smaller the boat, the more being out of trim will slow her down.

Never trim any vessel down by the head.

"Keep shifting your weight in a small sailing boat according to the puffs and lulls." Photo by Carol Singer. Courtesy, Sail magazine.

Trim a rowing boat slightly down by the stern, if anything. Don't let the stern of a sailing boat drag too much. Keep a small sailing boat heeled a little in a light air, and keep her as upright as you can in a breeze. Keep shifting your weight in a small sailing boat according to the puffs and lulls.

Take a board with you in a small sailing boat with thwarts, so you can move it all around between the thwarts and thus sit in an infinite number of positions to trim the boat just exactly right whatever the wind's vagaries.

Do not put any more weight than you have to in the ends of your vessel, else she will pitch unduly.

If you would keep your vessel going, give her a smooth bottom. Keep cleaning it off during the year; repaint if necessary. A boat with a rough or foul bottom can never do her best.

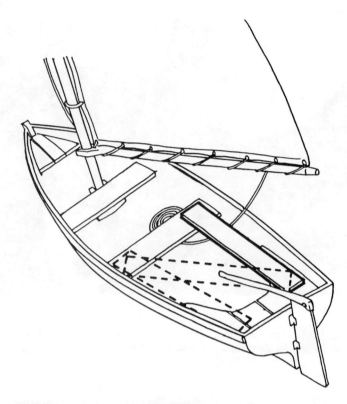

"Take a board with you in a small sailing boat with thwarts, so you can move it all around between the thwarts and thus sit in an infinite number of positions to trim the boat just exactly right whatever the wind's vagaries."

ENGINES

One way to keep a vessel going is with an engine. No mechanic, I can tell you everything I know about engines in just a few words.

Have a big engine that can move your vessel easily, not a tiny one that must strain all the time. An engine with power to spare is a much better shipmate than one that seems always to be wishing it had more horsepower.

Have your engine accessible. Right out in the cabin or cockpit is the best place for it. Next best is a nice, light, airy engine room with full headroom. The worst place for an engine is down in a deep, narrow bilge, covered over with various pieces of joinerwork.

Keep your engine clean.

Apply your senses to your engine while it is running. See the engine run; feel the engine run; hear the engine run; smell the engine run. If you sense trouble, such as seeing flames, feeling violent vibration, hearing parts flying about, or smelling smoke, shut her right down. If you act quickly enough, you may be able to save the engine to keep her going another day.

Never swear at your engine or kick it. Instead, reason logically and patiently with your engine. Remember that an engine is not a whimsical thing, but always obeys the laws of physics.

If an engine has fuel, air, and either a spark or compression, it must run.

Watch your gauges, check the cooling water coming out of your exhaust line, and best of luck.

If at all possible, give your propeller some protection. If the vessel should take the ground, you want something to hit bottom other than the propeller. Nor do you want stray underwater ropes to be able to get at it. Just as you give your vessel a smooth, clean bottom, give her a smooth, clean propeller. Before she goes overboard, polish it.

Carry as much fuel as you reasonably can in your vessel, and keep track of how much you have so that you don't run out.

Even if you are a mechanic who knows how to repair engines, still you may run up against a troubled machine that can only be cheered up with tools or parts that are far away on land. In such a situation, the more engines you have in your vessel, the better. The chance of two, three, or four engines simultaneously needing tools or spares that are not on board is remote.

OARS

An even more reliable way to keep a vessel going than with multiple engines is to row her along with oars. An oar may always break, I suppose, if you are too strenuous with it, but a spare oar is much easier to carry than is a spare engine.

If you would keep your vessel going under oars, have more than one pair. Have long, wide-tipped ones for smooth water or rowing with the wind when it's rough, and shorter, narrower-bladed ones for pulling against the wind or in a chop or seaway. It's a matter of gear ratio. Long oars are high-geared and give you plenty of speed under favorable conditions and in a light boat, but you have to pull hard on them. Shorter oars let you shift down and keep a heavy boat going in adverse conditions at a slower speed. The most common error in rowing is failing to take advantage of good conditions with long oars.

Have oars with considerable weight in the inner loom, so you don't have to waste energy holding the blades up out of the water on the return.

The key to why the oar works so well—as opposed to the mere paddle, for instance—is its fulcrum. Have smooth oarlocks just enough bigger than the oar leather to allow complete freedom of movement without unnecessary play. I was brought up to scorn circular oarlocks as indicating a lack of confidence in keeping the oar in, but have come to them in my dotage, now preferring convenience to reputation. The oar can't come out, and shipping oars and oarlocks is two operations instead of four. Of course you can't use a button (a shoulder on the leather to keep the oar from slipping out) with circular oarlocks unless you want to marry oar and oarlock forever.

Grease your oar leathers.

Keep her going under oars by taking it easy. No one stroke, however powerful, will get you very far. Be indifferent to every stroke while concentrating your attention on the miles.

Don't dig the blades in too deeply; barely submerged will do it. Pretend you are eating in high society; keep your elbows in. For a hard pull, use your back and legs more than your arms. Feather or not, according to your whim, and according to the conditions. Learn to feather well and smoothly for rowing against the wind. It's no use feathering on a long pull in a flat calm. Wide blades make good sails going with the wind, so you might as well trim them to advantage. Rowers who earn their living at a pair of oars feather very little.

You have to be mentally flexible when rowing across a steep chop. As the boat rolls, fixed notions about oar placement are argued away by the rapidly changing distance between extended oar blade and the water. This is the time for short oars. If, despite your best efforts, an oar blade you thought was about to be submerged gets rolled so high in the air you can't reach the water with it, abort that stroke and try another. Match your strokes to the waves in such conditions, not to the clock.

I had an elderly uncle who seemed to be able to keep his little skiff going to windward in a strong breeze without great effort. He used quick, tiny strokes, and his oar blades seemed always to be in the water. So when we children faced those conditions in our various boats, we would emulate him with "The Uncle Fred Taylor Stroke." It works.

If possible, have different rowing positions in your boat. After a few miles of sitting down and pulling and looking over your shoulder, it's a great relief to be able to stand up and push, slanting your oar blades, letting your weight fall forward on the oar handles, and watching where you're going without getting a kink in your neck. Now it seems so easy to keep her going that you feel as if you're cheating. But another mile or two and your back begins to weary of the recovery. Now it's a relief to sit down and pull again.

Pairs rowing is fun for going fast, but for a long pull, it's better for two people to swap off and stay fresh.

In a flat calm, you can keep a sizable sailing boat going

with an oar. If the boat displaces, say, over a ton, one oar seems to work better than two. Oars for big, heavy boats need to be long, and you quickly get to a size of oar too heavy and cumbersome for one person to row as a pair. On my 25-foot schooner, displacing just under two tons, one 12-foot oar seemed to work best. I could sit down and pull on it or stand up and push on it. Of course the helm had to be held over a bit to keep her going straight.

You can keep a boat going with a single oar by sculling. Again, slow and easy is the way to make progress. Now you want the oar blade well submerged. Start off by sculling with both hands, facing aft, to get yourself well into the figure-eight motion of the thing. Then, as soon as you've got the feel of it again and the boat is up to "speed," shift off to one hand, facing to starboard when sculling with the right hand, and to port with the left. Make yourself scull with the "wrong" hand as much as with the "right" hand until you can't remember which is which. If you can scull with either hand, you can stay fresh.

Sculling seems best for short distances in smooth water; it's a pipe-smoking sort of way to keep her going. Casual. My 12-foot oar worked fine sculling the little schooner in or out of the inner harbor in a calm.

SAILS

One of the nicest ways to keep your vessel going is by spreading sails to the breeze. To make good speed under sail, you need plenty of it. Do not skimp on your rig.

Have plenty of working sail area arranged to be easy to handle, and have plenty of big—even spectacular—light sails to keep her going when "there is not enough wind." Huge overlapping jibs and spinnakers will do wonders for a boat in light air. There's just no substitute for sail area if you would use the wind to keep her going.

In a hard breeze, drive her if you will, but remember that if your driving puts undue stress on the hull of your vessel,

"Have plenty of working sail area arranged to be easy to handle. There's just no substitute for sail area if you would use the wind to keep her going." Photo by Irving Nevells. Courtesy, National Fisherman.

"Sight along your spars to see that they stay straight."
Courtesy, Sail magazine.

you may suddenly have to forget all about keeping her
going and worry about keeping the water out. Also
remember that if your driving causes something to break—
such as a mast—your average speed will suddenly be
markedly reduced. It's fun to drive a boat a bit, but seldom
do sailors with the biggest reputation for driving have the
highest average lifetime speeds. Drive a boat with
moderation, if you know what I mean.

Sight along your spars to see that they stay straight.
Inspect your standing rigging.

Develop the habit of inspecting the details of your rig as
you sail along. Look for basic flaws. I'd hate to tack on a
rough night only to discover—too late—that a lee shroud—
now a weather one—was all adrift.

In rough weather, back up standing and running rigging

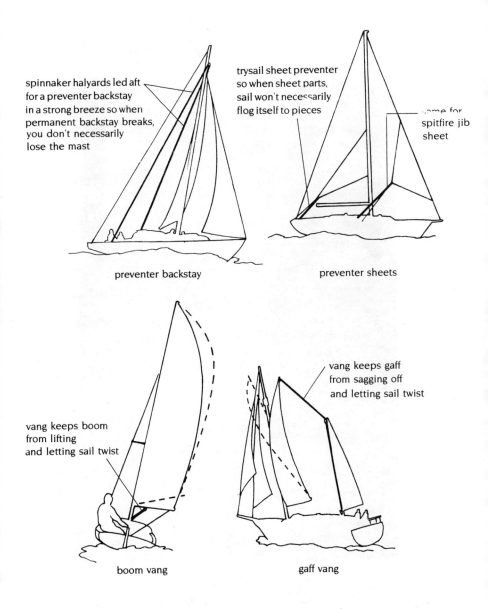

spinnaker halyards led aft
for a preventer backstay
in a strong breeze so when
permanent backstay breaks,
you don't necessarily
lose the mast

trysail sheet preventer
so when sheet parts,
sail won't necessarily
flog itself to pieces

same for
spitfire jib
sheet

preventer backstay

preventer sheets

vang keeps boom
from lifting
and letting sail twist

vang keeps gaff
from sagging off
and letting sail twist

boom vang

gaff vang

*"In rough weather, back up standing and running rigging with preventers,
duplicate pieces of rigging to take the strain if the primary piece should fail.
Use vangs on gaffs and booms to keep undue twist out of sails."*

with preventers, duplicate pieces of rigging to take the
strain if the primary piece should fail.

"Inspect running rigging often for chafe. It's hard to keep a vessel going once gear starts carrying away." Photo by Bill Beavis. Courtesy, Sail magazine.

Inspect running rigging and sails often for chafe. It's hard to keep a vessel going once gear starts carrying away.

Have flat working sails, not full ones. If you like to fool with changing the shape of your sails, by all means buy the new-fangled gear, such as bendy spars, hydraulic boom vangs, Cunninghams, and zippers. Just remember that when complicated gear breaks down at sea, your vessel will inevitably slow down.

When setting a gaff-rigged sail, peak it up until it wrinkles a bit from peak to tack while luffing. The wind will take the wrinkles out, and the more wind, the deeper the wrinkles it can smooth.

Keep your luffs set up hard. The more wind, the tighter the luff should be. Nothing helps a boat do her best to windward in a breeze more than setting up on her halyards. It's all right to use a hitch when belaying a halyard, but don't jam it. In squally weather, have your halyards all ready to cast off and run free.

Use vangs on gaffs and booms to keep undue twist out of sails.

When going to windward, don't trim sails in too hard; give them a little room to breathe. Never use a hitch when belaying a sheet.

On a reach, ease sheets all you can. Not-quite-luffing is the rule.

Keep the sag out of your headstays with fixed and running backstays well set up.

When trimming headsails, lead sheets to give approximately equal tension on foot and leech, but on no account let the leech be tighter than the foot.

Slightly overlapping sails will keep your vessel going faster than sails that don't overlap, and the difference in speed will be all out of proportion to the small extra sail area involved in the overlap.

Off the wind, don't let the sails blanket each other. Run wing-and-wing when you can, and rig preventers to keep from jibing. "Readin' both pages," the old-timers called it. Nice work, if you can get it.

One of the most useful and easily handled light sails is the balloon forestaysail on a boat with a double-head rig. It pulls well on a reach, can be poled out when running, and is easy to jibe.

"Get used to playing around with spinnakers. No sail is more fun. Let your spinnakers lift all they will and keep your clews level." Courtesy, Sail magazine.

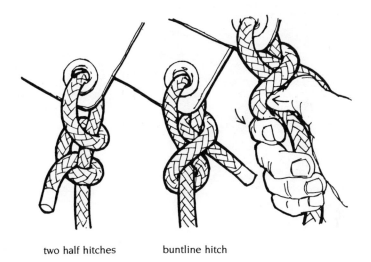

two half hitches   buntline hitch

Get used to playing around with spinnakers. No sail is more fun. Let your spinnakers lift all they will and keep your clews level.

Here's a great, simple surprisingly little-known knot for tying a sheet into the clew of a sail (and for many other uses). It's a square-rigger knot called the buntline hitch. It's just like two half hitches, but instead of piling one on top of the other, you make the first half hitch on the outside of the knot and the second one on the inside (see drawing). That way the end jams so the knot is much more secure than two half hitches, yet the outer hitch can be tipped down over the standing part to untie the knot easily, even when it's been under heavy strain. Learn to tie your half hitches "inside out."

Don't be afraid to experiment with the trim of your sails. On the other hand, don't experiment so much that your vessel never gets a chance to settle down and really get going.

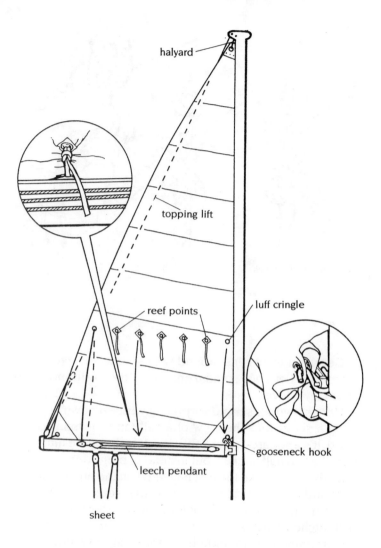

halyard

topping lift

reef points

luff cringle

gooseneck hook

leech pendant

sheet

To reef: 1. Take up on topping lift. 2. Slack away on halyard. 3. Trim sheet in hard. 4. Hook luff cringle on gooseneck hook. 5. Heave away on leech pendant. 6. Tie reef points around foot of sail (not around boom). 7. Ease sheet. 8. Set up halyard. 9. Slack topping lift. 10. Trim sheet to suit.

If you are fortunate enough to have a centerboard, don't forget to pull it up off the wind. In a small boat, leave a little board down to help keep control of things when running in a fresh breeze.

As it breezes on, shorten down early. As it moderates, clap on more sail early.

On the wind, when the rail of your vessel begins going under consistently in the puffs, it's time to shorten down. If your boat is so high-sided that you never get the great sensation of speed that comes with sailing her rail-down, I suppose you have to tell when to shorten down by a red mark on an inclinometer. Off the wind, shorten down early enough so that if you had to bring her on the wind, she wouldn't be overpowered. This is usually sooner than you think.

When shortening down going to windward, keep your sail plan balanced; take off as much sail forward as you do aft. When shortening down off the wind, take off more sail aft than you do forward. Leave a good headsail on her to hold her head off and ease the helm.

Rigs and sail combinations abound in great variety, but most vessels have mainsails, and, with most rigs, the first thing to do when shortening down is to reef the mainsail. Have plenty of reefs in your mainsail, a couple of shallow ones for fine adjustment in a fresh breeze and deeper ones so you can reef away much of the sail when it's really blowing hard.

If the leech cringle of a reef is hard to reach, keep its pendant all rove off. Keep your reefing pendants handy, and don't be tempted to use them for anything else. A heavy hook at the gooseneck for the luff cringle makes sense. Reef points are much handier to use than a laceline that has to be rove through reefing eyelets. Reef luff, then leech; shake out leech, then luff.

Stout topping lifts and a thick web of lazyjacks help reefing without taking the sail all the way down.

Roller-reefing gear on a mainsail gives infinite adjustment, but the sail doesn't keep its shape as well as when you tie in a reef. If you have roller-reefing gear, have a couple of sets of reefing cringles and eyelets to use when the gear fails.

There may come a time when you want to haul a sail down in a hurry. Rig downhauls on your sails. For sails that set on masts, a simple downhaul rig is to tie the bitter end of the halyard into the first cringle below the head of the sail with a bowline (not the head itself, which could result in a jam) and send it aloft when you hoist the sail.* Then you have a way to pull down directly on the head of the sail with all your weight if necessary. On headsails, rig a separate line from the first cringle below the head of the sail through a lead block at the foot of the stay and aft to a convenient belaying point.

If you need to get a sail down fast and no downhaul is rigged, haul down on the luff of the sail. One night in the Gulf Stream, a squall carried away the jib sheet on the 71-foot yawl *Royono*. The people forward immediately let go the jib halyard and started to claw the sail down, but by the time I had made my way from the cockpit to the end of the bowsprit, the thrashing sail was still very much up. Pulling down on the sail's luff proved much more effective than clawing at the sail's belly.

To keep her going temporarily in a squall, you can scandalize a gaff mainsail by setting up on the topping lift and then slacking the peak halyard right off so that the whole peak of the sail drops behind and is blanketed by what becomes a nice trysail from throat to clew. A vang on the gaff comes in handy for this tactic. Catboat people, especially, love to sail scandalously through squalls this way.

Roller-furling headsails have the great advantage that

---

*You'll doubtless remember that on my skipjack the bitter end of the main halyard was tied into the head cringle. I could get away with that because a skipjack's rig necessitates considerable distance from head cringle to the next cringle down, so you can pull on the very head without jamming anything.

they can be taken in fast. They are frustrating when they don't work. They are dangerous if they unroll in a squall.

Don't use headsails (or mainsails, for that matter) whose luffs slide into grooves unless you have a large crew that likes extra work.

In most boats with a double-head rig, it is the forestaysail, not the jib, that should come in first when you need to shorten down the headsail area. Taking the staysail in first changes the boat's balance less than taking the jib in first.

Keep a headsail on if you possibly can when shortening down. A boat with no headsail (other than a catboat) isn't going to keep going very well.

Have a tiny, strong trysail and a tiny, strong spitfire jib. With these sails, you can keep her going even in a real breeze. The smaller the boat, the more necessary are these tiny sails. It's amazing how much breeze a small, open boat will stand—and how fast she'll go—under a tiny "traveling" sail.

TRICKS OF THE TRADE

Have a good barometer and watch it. Have a good radio, and listen to it for storm warnings. Rely more on your own weather observations than on the predictions of a shorebound radio announcer who talks to you from a room without windows. Don't worry too much about predicting the weather; people have been at it for years with little success. Rather, be ready for all kinds of weather—the sure prediction is that they're all coming your way sooner or later—and be prepared to keep her going through their endless variety.

Let wind and tide set your schedule if at all possible. Give yourself a fair wind and a fair tide every chance you get.

Watch the wind closely. Just the other day, sailing a

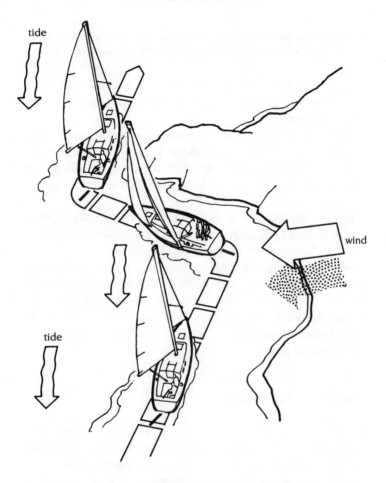

"Cheat a foul tide all you can. Work in behind a point to keep out of it. Put it on your lee bow, so it will both set you up to windward and increase your apparent wind."

dinghy out of the harbor, I was having a brush with a couple of much bigger boats. We were working up to windward in a light air from the north. Looking out across the bay, I saw boats heeling to a moderate southerly and immediately gave up working to windward in favor of running off to try to be the first one to catch the new breeze when it arrived. It worked.

It's rare, though, that you want to give up your advantage of being up to windward—weather gauge. Nearly every time, it pays to be a little pessimistic and hold to windward of where you want to go. Money in the bank. When things go wrong, weather gauge is priceless.

Cheat a foul tide all you can. Work in behind a point to keep out of it. Put it on your lee bow, so it will both set you up to windward and increase your apparent wind.

Don't gamble with long tacks. There's nothing more discouraging than sailing close-hauled for miles, only to have the wind shift and put you right back where you started.

Sail in smooth water, up under the land, if you can.

When trying to work to windward in a light air with a leftover sea, ease sheets, fill her well away, get her going, and then bring her gradually back up close-hauled. If you don't try to head too high, it's amazing how well you can keep her going in such frustrating conditions using this tactic. When running off in such conditions, keep her up enough to fill her headsails.

To get the most out of a following sea, shoot diagonally across it, like a surfer.

In rough weather, run her off to change sails. Sometimes the best way to keep her going is to be easy on vessel and crew.

In rough weather, tack a small boat; don't jibe her. Watch for a smooth before you tack. In heavy weather, wear a big vessel; don't tack her.

Don't sail by the lee for any distance. Jibe her over and be done with it; then jibe again if you have to.

When steering a vessel under sail, sit to windward. Watch the waves and steer round the worst of them if it's rough. Watch the tiny little ripples all over the tops of the waves to learn the wind direction with precision. Watch for the darkness of closely spaced ripples to learn about approaching puffs and gusts. Feel the wind direction and strength on your face or the back of your neck. Sense the heel of the boat. Sense her speed through the water. All these things tell you how to steer and how well you are

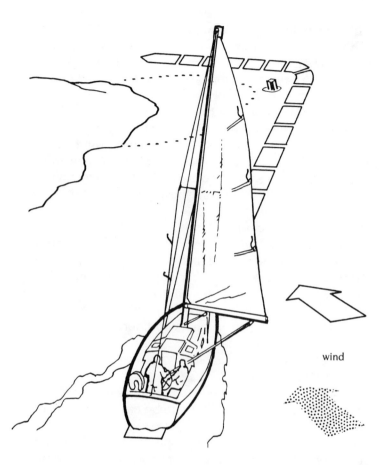

wind

"Don't sail by the lee for any distance. Jibe her over and be done with it; then jibe again if you have to." (In this example, it's time to jibe; then jibe again at the buoy.)

doing by the vessel. If you sit to leeward to watch the jib, you'll lose much of this information.

Waves and the tiny ripples and the feel of the wind and the heel and speed of the boat let you anticipate whether she needs to be headed up a little or headed off a little to do her best. Use as little rudder as possible.

Sailing to windward is a continuous experiment to see
how much you can get away with. Keep her up all you can,
but keep her footing. Remember that the wind is changing
continuously in direction and strength. Keep one eye on
the luff of your mainsail. Don't let it shake in a light breeze;
keep it just lifting in a moderate breeze; and let it bulge to
ease her if you have to in a strong breeze.

Don't starve a boat for wind. Bring her up all you can, but
the instant you sense her faltering, keep her away again a
little and give her back her breeze. The better the
conditions—moderate breeze, flat sea—the higher you can
point and still keep her footing fast.

Don't tack any faster than you have to to get her well
around without losing too much way. In smooth water in a
gentle breeze, take full advantage of shooting to windward
during a tack.

In light weather, move around your vessel like a cat. The
smaller the boat, the more stamping and jumping will slow
her down.

You can keep your vessel going with combinations of
engine and sail or oar and sail. The possible variations are
infinite. I like to think of a twin-screw motorsailer working
to windward under sail with her lee engine ticking over to
help her along. Or a dinghy running up a river on the last of
the evening breeze, with somebody helping her along with
an oar, rowed languidly.

How fast will she go? Hull speed—the maximum speed
of a hull before wave-making energy goes right off the
graph—may be expressed by a constant multiplied by the
square root of the waterline length of the vessel. For hulls
of "average fineness" ("normal" wave-making characteristics), the constant would be about 1.3. Running down a
following sea will give momentary speeds higher than hull
speed, but average speed in a following sea—unless you
can surf or plane—will be lower than the speed you'd get
from the same breeze in smooth water.

"When steering a vessel under sail, sit to windward. Feel the wind direction and strength on your face or the back of your neck. Sense the heel of the boat. Sense her speed through the water. All these things tell you how to steer and how well you are doing by the vessel." Photo by Brian Manby. Courtesy, Sail *magazine.*

There's one kind of day when it's really not much fun to try to keep her going. This is the sparkling day when there's a gusty, fluky land breeze and everybody says, "Oh, what a wonderful day to go sailing!" Don't you believe it. These land breezes are treacherous and frustrating. There's no

"If you sit to leeward to watch the jib, you'll lose much of this information."
Courtesy, National Fisherman.

way to keep her going in such a breeze. It might be better to brush on some varnish at the mooring.

Speaking of which, in the next chapter, we'll talk about keeping her where you want her.

4

Keeping Her Where You Want Her

Anchor, Hardy, anchor!

Horatio Nelson after Trafalgar

For every vessel but one, an element of seamanship is the ability to stop traveling and stay put for a while. A vessel is made to go voyaging, of course, but on occasion, you must keep her where you want her, a feat not altogether simple, as you can tell by watching a boat tug at her tethers. Only the *Flying Dutchman* need not bother with this element of seamanship.

Sometimes it is simply a matter of keeping her where you want her long enough to delay the end of the voyage. Once in the Herreshoff Newport 29 *Mischief*, we had been powering all night through a calm, heading down Delaware Bay to enter the harbor at Cape May through its back-door creek. We didn't want to go in in the dark, because we weren't absolutely positive our mast was going to fit under the creek's fixed bridge. So we kept her where we wanted her, off the mouth of the creek, for a couple of hours awaiting the dawn.

It was my watch, so I got to decide how to do this.

Just as I started thinking about the problem, a moderate breeze sprang up, the first wind we had felt since leaving Annapolis and bringing her through the Chesapeake and Delaware Canal. So I put on full sail and had a grand time roaring back and forth on a reach maybe a mile in each direction.

The more normal tactic, though, would be to keep the vessel just jogging along slowly. Easy when under power or rowing: just cut way back on revolutions or strokes. For jogging under sail, have a much-reduced, balanced rig. The schooner's foresail is ideal. Set a main trysail with other rigs, or a tiny traveling sail in a dinghy.

Stop your vessel out on the water sometimes, just for the sheer peace and pleasure of the thing. Stop for the occasional meal—or even just for tea. (Someday, I'm going to take the ideal vacation cruise: sail offshore, drift for a week, and then sail home again.) There is nothing so peaceful as a vessel intentionally drifting.

DRIFTING, LYING-TO, AND HEAVING-TO

Nothing could be easier than letting a vessel drift. Stop the engine; ship the oars; hand the sails. Watch her drift. No longer is she attacking waves or trying to keep up with them. Now she's just giving to them. Ahhh.

If you want to stop under sail without bothering to take all the sails down, let fly your sheets with the boat close-hauled, and then, when she has coasted to a stop, put the helm all the way down so that if she pays off and gets a bit of wind in her sails, the rudder will head her right back up again as soon as she gets any headway. Dropping headsails helps this tactic.

One time sailing singlehanded in the Herreshoff Buzzards Bay 25-footer *Aria*, lack of foresight and a dumb decision forced me to stop her right in the rough entrance between the jetties at Point Judith's Harbor of Refuge to get the jib off. I let everything fly, rounded her up, and went forward to do the job. By the time I had finished, she was lying quietly, lifting to the seas where she had stopped, waiting patiently for me to take her in behind the breakwater.

In a sharpie, with no standing rigging, you don't even have to bring her up to close-hauled. Just let the sheets fly any old time on any point of sailing. Wonderful vessels, sharpies.

Don't get totally mesmerized by your drifting vessel. Remember that wind and tide are taking you slowly over the bottom in some direction at a slow speed; eventually you must navigate.

If, instead of merely drifting, you wish to lie-to with your vessel's head to wind, you can convert your boat into a weather vane by setting a sail aft, strapping it down, and lashing your helm amidships. Now she'll go pretty much straight astern, though at a faster rate than when drifting with the wind abeam.

The mizzen of a yawl or ketch makes a fine sail for lying-to, and a schooner's mainsail works well if her mainmast is not too far forward. A cutter, sloop, or catboat needs a small riding sail set up temporarily on backstay or topping lift.

If keeping her where you want her involves avoiding leeway, heave-to. Try backing a headsail against filled after sails with the vessel close-hauled and helm alee. The backed headsail will kill most of her headway and will hold her head off against the rudder trying to round her up. In a centerboard boat, you can fool with the board to help get her balanced just right.

Anytime you are drifting, lying-to, or hove-to, pay close attention to the unusual strains these maneuvers may put on your rudder.

Wind

"Try backing a headsail against filled after sails with the vessel close-hauled and helm alee. The backed headsail will kill most of her headway and will hold her head off against the rudder trying to round her up."

You can use a sea anchor to help keep your vessel where you want her. The biggest problem with a sea anchor is designing it to create enough drag really to hold the vessel. One of the best sea anchors is a real anchor let out with lots of scope; the anchor holds the rode down at an angle so that the vessel has to drag it more or less sideways through the water. This kind of sea anchor has the great advantage that if the vessel comes onto soundings, it will fetch up on something and convert itself back into an ordinary anchor.

ANCHORING

It is the real anchor, of course, that is used most to keep a voyaging vessel where you want her, usually in protected water of your choice.

Choose your anchorages with care and imagination. When seeking protection, imagine the wind blowing from all points of the compass. Don't tuck in too close under a weather shore lest later it becomes a lee shore. Anchor in plenty of water, and allow for the fall of the tide. Try to pick good holding ground. Try to give yourself plenty of swinging room so you can let out all the scope you want.

Under sail, enter an anchorage along its lee side, giving yourself lots of room to head up to windward and slow her down. Notice how other vessels are lying to their anchors so you can judge where your vessel will end up in relation to where you drop your anchor. Don't anchor too close to other vessels; don't hesitate to ask other vessels to move should they anchor too close to you.

If, when your vessel settles back on her anchor line all secure, you look around and really don't like your berth— maybe she didn't end up just where you planned—you'll be a lot happier if you pick up the anchor right then and move it to where you want it than if you spend your whole time at anchor saying to yourself, "I wish I were over *there*." If you have anchored in the wrong spot, swallow your pride and go anchor in the right spot.

Or, if, after you've anchored, you begin to feel uneasy about your vessel's situation, if there is something you can do to make her more secure, do it. Once, cruising with a gang in a schooner, I ran right through a perfectly nice harbor and was determined to take her as far as possible up a narrow, tide-ridden tickle. It sure was wild and beautiful up in there, but the minute the anchor went down, I started to worry. She lay in three knots of current at the strength of the tide, first pulling on the anchor one way, then the opposite way. If she pulled her anchor out, she'd be onto that pretty shore in no time. I should have said, "Sorry, folks, we're going back out into the harbor." Instead, I spent the next twelve hours worrying.

If your vessel is so large that anchoring her requires communication between bow and stern, use hand signals to say clearly, "Come left," or "Come right," or "Back her down," or "Let go." Never shout, "Shall I drop it?" or scream, "Over there more!"

Drop your anchors, don't throw them. Let them have scope as the vessel draws it out with her way; don't drop slack anchor cable on top of an anchor or it may get foul.

Wait for the vessel to lose all way before letting go. Then let her sternway draw out the scope.

If she gets much sternway, snub her and use it to set the anchor. If there is not enough wind to give her much sternway, set the anchor with a good hard heave on the rode. Of course a vessel with power can set her anchor by backing down on it.

If, under sail, you don't have room to round up and get her stopped where you want to let go the anchor, you can drop it where you want it with headway, veer out a reasonable amount of scope, and then use the anchor to stop her. Then let her drift back to where she will lie, but remember to set the anchor as usual, once she's settled into her berth. A flying moor, the old-timers called it, and they only used it when they had to.

Always attach some sort of anchor cable to your anchor before dropping it. I have never known a real case of this rule being broken, but sailors being no less absentminded than anyone else, I suppose it must have happened. Don't unbend anchor cables from anchors without good reason.

Be observant when anchoring. I recently read what was presented as a true story about somebody who let go an anchor off his bowsprit, veered plenty of scope, and was surprised that it didn't seem to be holding his vessel at all. When he finally got around to looking over the bow, there was his anchor hanging on his bobstay by a fluke.

Sense what's happening with your hands as well as with your eyes. Grab your straining rode and feel whether or not its anchor is sending vibrations to the vessel. An anchor that isn't budging sends no vibrations. A dragging anchor sends irregular vibrations with a taut urgency to them that lets you distinguish them from the slacker, regular vibrations currents can produce in the catenary of a cable.

Though the anchor is the symbol of hope, try to replace hope with certainty insofar as is possible when keeping your vessel where you want her with ground tackle. If you would sleep well at anchor, use big anchors, let out plenty of scope, and put on chafing gear.

Any anchor, no matter how well designed, needs considerable weight if it is to hold. Don't skimp on the size of your anchors. If your vessel's hull design lets her sail around her anchor a lot, give her extra big anchors, for she's always trying to wrench them out.

Most any vessel deserves more than one anchor, most deserve three, and a sizable vessel that will depend on her ground tackle often will put a choice of four to good use.

Anchor number one is stowed on the bow, as ready as possible for instant letting go. This anchor should be big enough to hold the vessel in anything short of a gale.

Anchor number two is a sheet anchor, an anchor that surely *is* big enough to hold the vessel, gale or not. This monster may be stowed amidships on deck, or disassembled and stowed below, maybe even in the bilge. Knowledge of its being on board, ready to be set up, shackled on, and struggled overboard in a hard chance, is a great comfort.

Anchor number three can be a light anchor for light work, such as holding her against the tide in a calm, keeping her where you want her briefly in light weather, or holding her stern where you want it.

Anchor number four might be a medium-sized anchor of a different design from the others for use on a specific type of bottom.

You can't have too many anchors. It's a great thing always to have another anchor you can put out.

The most versatile anchor is the yachtsman type, or fisherman or old-fashioned anchor, as it is sometimes called. It will hold best under the indifferent anchoring conditions you often meet, such as poor holding ground or insufficient swinging room to let out all the scope you want.

Next best is the CQR, or plow anchor. This anchor holds well except on a rocky bottom or with short scope.

The Danforth anchor is a good choice for anchor number four. It has tremendous holding power for its weight, given good anchoring conditions. To live up to its fantastic reputation, it needs a steady pull from one direction with plenty of scope.

Don't use lightweight seaplane anchors on boats; they make as much sense as lead keels on seaplanes.

Help your anchors hold by pulling on them as nearly horizontally as possible. The more scope you can let out, the more nearly horizontal will be the pull of the rode. Judge your scope by veering rode until it makes a nice flat angle with the water. An anchor rode in a boat of any size at all ought to be at least 200 feet long. Carry long rodes.

Weight on the rode, down near the anchor, helps. This can be a length of chain, also good to prevent chafe should the rode encounter a sharp rock or obstruction on the bottom. You can send a separate weight down the anchor rode, sliding on a shackle with a messenger line to retrieve it, to help keep the pull horizontal. Such an extra weight, or the extra weight of a length of chain shackled to the anchor, is particularly effective in reducing the disadvantage of a necessarily short scope.

Perhaps the most effective way to add weight to the rode down near the anchor is with another anchor. I've just recently gotten onto this tandem anchoring business, and I'm so excited about it I now always put two anchors overboard on one rode. I'm convinced the total weight of ground tackle can be less with this system. A good combination, for instance, is a length of chain, then a

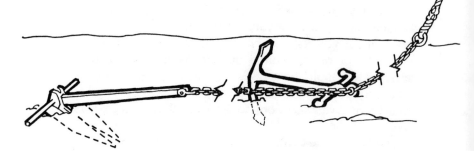

"A good combination is a length of chain, then a yachtsman's anchor, then another length of chain, then a Danforth."

yachtsman's anchor, then another length of chain, then a Danforth. The chains give weight and prevent chafe, and the yachtsman's gives the Danforth the perfect holding conditions it craves. I estimate this combination is worth a yachtsman's anchor of double the weight of the whole conglomeration.

Your anchor cable ought to have some give to it so that when the vessel pitches in a seaway, the heavy strain on the rode of the bow lifting won't be transmitted directly to the anchor. Some sailors like the big, heavy catenary of an all-chain cable to produce the necessary give; others like a rode made of stretchy rope, such as nylon. If you have all-chain cable, have also a rope cable for rowing out an extra anchor.

When making fast the rode to the ring of an anchor, use the anchor bend, with its extra turn through the ring. Leave a nice long end so you can clap on plenty of half hitches with it. No use having it come untied. If the rode will stay on the anchor a long time, you might as well seize the end back onto the standing part with marlin.

Wire your shackle pins so they can't come unscrewed and bend the sharp ends of the wire back inside the shackles where they won't catch or chafe on things. Grease your shackle pins and then set up hard on them.

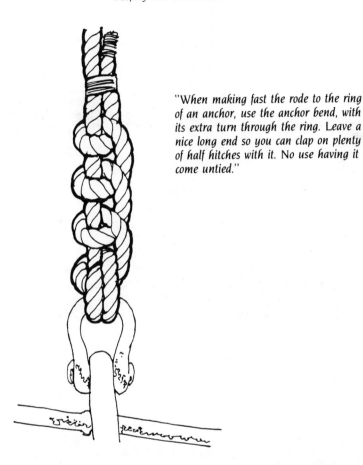

"When making fast the rode to the ring of an anchor, use the anchor bend, with its extra turn through the ring. Leave a nice long end so you can clap on plenty of half hitches with it. No use having it come untied."

Have something stout on the foredeck to make the anchor cable fast to. The best thing is a nice big pair of bitts or a samson post going right down into the vessel's backbone. Cleats ought to be bolted through something heavy. All this stuff ought to be plenty big. Remember that in a hard chance, your mast may be the best deck gear you have for making fast the anchor cable.

Catch a turn round post or cleat when veering anchor rode, a couple of turns if the strain will be heavy when you hold it. The strain that comes on an anchor rode when you hold it is usually more than you think it will be.

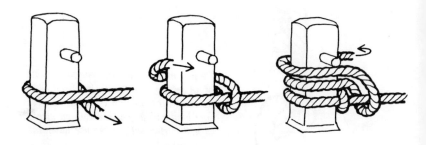

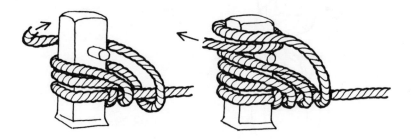

Above: "On a post, use the towboat hitch, rather than a clove hitch."
Below: "Have big, smooth bow chocks." Courtesy, National Fisherman.

Make an anchor rode fast to a cleat with a hitch. On a post, use the towboat hitch, rather than a clove hitch.

If you secure the bitter end of an anchor cable below in the forepeak, make it *secure* and use line accessible to a knife.

Have big, smooth bow chocks. Lash the rode down into them if she's pitching. Use chafing gear on an anchor rode where it bears on a bobstay. In a rough anchorage, keep freshening the nip where your anchor rode goes through the chock.

Anchors sometimes get fouled; that is, the rode catches a turn around some part of the anchor so it's then pulling on that part instead of on the ring. For instance, the rode may wrap around the up-ended, lazy fluke of a dug-in yachtsman's anchor if wind and tide send the vessel round her anchor without pulling on it. If fluky conditions do this to your vessel, sight the anchor, that is, bring it to the surface momentarily to see that it's not foul.

If you pull on a Danforth anchor from one direction and then pull on it from the opposite direction, heavy clay or a stone that it may have picked up can prevent the flukes from swinging by the stock when the anchor tips over, so the flukes won't dig in again. Another case where sighting the anchor is well worth the trouble.

When anchored in your vessel, be alert to any change of motion. Sense what's going on around you. Once we were having breakfast in the 43-foot double-ended Alden yawl *Hostess* in Burnt Coat Harbor, Swan's Island, Maine, when something went wrong with the tiny view out the porthole. A mast presented itself where no mast should be. We popped on deck and sure enough, our Danforth had broken right out and we were underway.

When anchored in adverse conditions, stand anchor watches. You may not need to watch over your vessel continuously, the way you do when she is underway, but you ought to be taking a good look around every few minutes to be sure she's not dragging. If everybody is sleeping in at anchor on a quiet night, and you happen to wake up, stick your head out the hatch to see what's going on.

As it gets dark, notice the bearings of some prominent all-night lights.

If your anchor drags, veer more cable. Have a second anchor ready to put overboard. If there's room to leeward, you may want to drop it quickly right underfoot and then keep veering on both rodes. If you don't have room to leeward, row the second anchor out to windward. If you think back on most of the times you've put out a second anchor, you'll probably realize that you should have put it out earlier. It's a lot easier to put out a second anchor and not need it than to put it out after you've discovered you jolly well do need it.

Hang a heavy anchor from the stern of your dinghy when carrying it out. Make the rode fast on the vessel at a point that will give you a lot more scope than you need. Take all that scope with you in the dinghy, coiled carefully into the little boat so it will pull clear as you row out. That way you won't have to pull the rode off the vessel and through the water as you row into the wind and chop. Lay your second anchor some distance away from the first so that when you even up the strain on the rodes you'll have one on either bow. Now your second anchor is not only increasing your holding power, but also keeping the direction of pull relatively constant.

To break out an anchor after it has been keeping your vessel where you want her, pull on it vertically. Just as anchors love that horizontal pull because it keeps them well dug in, they hate that vertical pull, which just as surely must break their grip on the bottom.

Even so, an anchor may be so well dug in after a gale that it is hard to break out when heaving round with the rode up and down. In such a situation, take full advantage of any surge. When the boat's bow falls a little, take right up hard on the rode and hold it; when her bow lifts a little, you'll be hauling up on the anchor with tremendous force.

If you must anchor in foul ground where you are afraid a

fluke may become permanently wedged under a rock or some debris, tie a tripping line to the crown of your yachtsman's anchor, either buoying it or tying it off, with some slack, on the rode. You'd have to be mighty unlucky not to be able to retrieve an anchor by heaving round on a tripping line to its crown.

Anchoring is a wonderful business. Some of the best times in a boat are coming to anchor and getting underway from an anchor, because both events are filled with anticipation.

MOORING

To keep your vessel where you want her in your home port, use a heavy mooring with heavy chain and a heavy mooring pendant well laced with chafing gear. When the wind rattles the windows of your house at night, it's good to know that out in the harbor your vessel is lying to mighty strong stuff.

Your vessel ought to be able to lift her own mooring for inspection. Use the tide to break it out.

A mushroom anchor makes the best mooring in any bottom that's not unduly hard. Put a tripping chain on your mushroom. Bore a hole near the edge of the bowl, put in an eyebolt, and shackle the tripping chain to it, wiring the upper end of the tripping chain, with slack, into the main mooring chain high enough up so you can get the tripping chain on board easily at low water. Taking a strain on the tripping chain when you need to lift your mooring will tip the mushroom over and break it out relatively easily. For a mooring on hard bottom, use a huge old-fashioned anchor with the upper fluke sawed off so the anchor can't get foul.

A couple of anchors bridled together makes a good mooring. Use swivels on mooring chains and wire your shackle pins.

When leaving the vessel on her mooring, lash the eye of

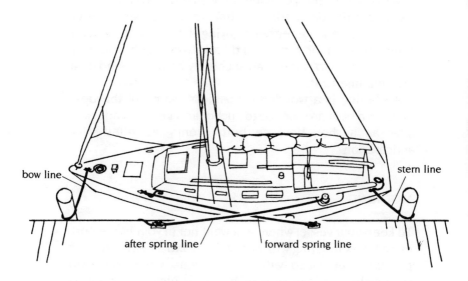

bow line *stern line* *after spring line* *forward spring line*

"If you need to bring her alongside, add a stern line and a couple of springs."

the mooring pendant down to something with a lashing as strong as the pendant itself, in case the eye should somehow get off its post or cleat. Pass the lashing through the eye, not around it.

To moor a boat in shallow water, drive in a big stake, and tie her up to it with a clove hitch backed by a half hitch.

If a hurricane threatens, run your vessel way up some narrow gunkhole and take your anchor cables ashore to the toughest medium-sized trees you can find.

Perhaps the simplest way of all of keeping your vessel where you want her is to let her take the bottom intentionally. The flat-bottomed boat has it all over any other type, of course, for this sort of work. Let the tide set your vessel down on fairly smooth, even bottom when grounding her out. Watch out for rocks.

If your vessel doesn't have a flat bottom (or twin keels), make a set of legs to be lashed alongside her and hold her upright when on the hard.

When beaching a small boat to keep her where you want her, pull her well up above the high-tide mark and make her painter fast to something permanent. If you would cure yourself forever of casualness in this matter, read L.S. Hall's "The Ledge" in *Tales from the Skipper.*

When using a dock to keep your vessel where you want her, choose the lee side if possible. Let her lie off on a bow line. If you need to bring her alongside, add a stern line and a couple of springs. Allow for the fall of the tide. Use bowlines or back clove hitches with half hitches.

Remember that when you step ashore from your vessel onto a dock, you are stepping ashore to your seaman's reputation. In the next chapter, we'll talk about how to keep it.

5

Keeping
Your
Reputation

A man who is not afraid of the sea will soon be drownded, he said, for he will be going out on a day he shouldn't. But we do be afraid of the sea, and we do only be drownded now and again.

J.M. *Synge, in* The Aran Islands

My father already had something of a seaman's reputation by the time he graduated from the U.S. Naval Academy. Somebody wrote of him in the 1906 *Lucky Bag* that he "could sail a catboat over Niagara Falls without shipping a sea."

He got this sort of reputation through early exposure to a variety of kinds of rowing and sailing craft that he operated—often under the expert tutelage of an older brother whose seaman's reputation exceeded his own—in waters ranging from quiet, sandy, salt ponds to the rough, old ocean. Uncle Fred made Pop do things right on the water and gave him to understand that if he got himself into a lash-up in a boat, he would be expected to get himself out of it.

Pop brought me up the same way, teaching both basics and fine points by example and landing on me pretty hard whenever I messed up.

The system has worked for millennia; the able-bodied seaman teaches the apprentice seaman. If the lessons are true sea lessons, they are laced with the fear of being "drownded."

If you are an apprentice seaman, find an able-bodied seaman to teach you. If you are an able-bodied seaman, find yourself an apprentice seaman to teach.

From the first time you step in a boat, you are building your seaman's reputation. It's a precious thing, hard and long to build, easy and quick to lose.

Take pride in your seaman's reputation. Steer carefully, getting the best out of your vessel and keeping a good course. Take pride in your rowing. Keep your vessel shipshape and Bristol fashion with no loose ends.

Scrutinize photographs of vessels. What's the head of that jib doing luffing? Why doesn't he ease his mizzen topping lift? Look at the smoke she's making. If somebody took a photograph of your boat now, would it stand up to scrutiny?

One element of a seaman's reputation is the way he balances caution and boldness. One good sailor may have a reputation for shortening down drastically whenever it looks like blowing; another, equally good, may have a reputation for being a big sail carrier. Neither is necessarily right or wrong. Personality comes into play, as does the purpose of being underway. A voyage of pleasure, profit, training, or rescue each ought to have its own standards of daring. You can visualize situations in which only the foolhardy would risk getting underway in a strong breeze, yet others in which only a fool would refuse to face a whole gale.

Victor Hugo made the point well in *The Toilers of the Sea*:

> Sieur Clubin, although he had rather the look of a notary than of a sailor, was a mariner of rare skill. He had all the talents which are required to meet dangers of every kind. He was a skillful stower, a safe man aloft, an able and careful boatswain, a powerful steersman, an experienced pilot, and a bold captain. He was prudent, and he carried his prudence sometimes to the point of daring, which is a great quality at sea. His natural apprehensiveness of danger was tempered by a strong instinct of what was possible in an emergency. He was one of those mariners who will face risks to a point perfectly well known to themselves, and who generally managed to come successfully out of every peril. Every certainty which a man can command, dealing with so fickle an element as the sea, he possessed.

Luck plays a vital role in your seaman's reputation. The sea may happen to allow great feats of seamanship, but it can also, next time out, destroy the best of seamen and their vessels. It is not with impunity that we go on the water, but with sufferance. Good seamen help their luck, like the master of the old coasting schooner mending his hatch tarpaulins in fair weather.

Some sailors always seem to have a fair wind and a fair tide. Luck is at work here too, certainly, but so also are flexibility and patience.

Keep your reputation by the diligent use of imagination and foresight. Before a difficult—or even a simple—maneuver, sit down and figure out the best way to do it, what things can go wrong with it, and what you'll do then. Make your preparations methodically, step by step. Don't be in any more hurry than you have to be.

Don't be mesmerized by the familiarity of a simple maneuver. Not long ago, I ran into the harbor and rounded up to lay my little schooner alongside a float. To be sure, the landing would be on a bit of a "lee shore," but nothing could be simpler. The thought crossed my mind—I remembered later that it actually occurred to me—that I might as well let the jib sheet go early, before I made my half circle round into the wind to go alongside. But then, somehow, I didn't bother, because it all seemed so utterly easy. The next thing I know, I am approaching the float with the mainsail luffing and the jib just as full of wind as you please, keeping her going and paying her head right off. By the time I did let the jib go and get the little mainsail backed out for a brake, a person on the boat who luckily was not in the least mesmerized by the situation jumped forward and fended off smartly, otherwise there would have been splinters.

Let us learn from our mistakes.

Before maneuvering, tell people what you are going to do and how you are going to do it—even why. (Had I done this in the aforementioned example, I would have been forced to explain to myself, while explaining to the others, the importance of not having any wind in the jib as we ranged alongside the float.)

Keep your reputation by inspecting and observing everything on your vessel. Notice parts of the rig and gear, what is coming adrift, what is led foul, and what needs a lashing.

Take precautions. Rig preventers. Expect things to go wrong.

Keep up with events; don't procrastinate. Do make the anchor ready well ahead of time. Do have the crew practice skipper-overboard drills. Do put the cover on the jam jar before tacking.

Keep your reputation by dealing well with emergencies. Be alert to an accident happening and be quick as a cat to react to prevent it or recover from it. In a boat, one accident can lead to another very quickly, so break the chain as early as possible. Yet don't be afraid to do nothing in a difficult situation until you have figured out what is really best to do. For instance, if your mast should come crashing down on deck, instantly yell and shove and jump to try to prevent injury, but then calm right down. After all, no water is

"If your mast should come crashing down on deck, instantly yell and shove and jump to try to prevent injury, but then calm right down. It's merely a question of setting priorities, and working through the mess step by step." Photo by Colin Jarman. Courtesy, Sail magazine.

coming in, and you haven't hit anything. It's merely a question of setting priorities, and working through the mess step by step. When Pop lost his mast once, as soon as the excitement was over, the first thing he did was go below and make some coffee.

Do enough physical work to stay in reasonable shape. In particular, don't let your hands get too soft. There are times when you'll want a grip like pliers and fingers like marlinspikes.

Keep your vessel simple, but carry plenty of basic supplies and spares. Have a knife handy, and keep it

"Keep your systems for propulsion, fuel, cooking, and heating from catching on fire. Keep these systems tight, and keep them clean." Photo by Jane Day. Courtesy, National Fisherman.

sharp. Worry about breaking unique and valuable gear like your compass or your sextant.

Move about slowly on your vessel with patience rather than haste. Be particularly careful below in a seaway.

Have a doctor, complete with black bag, on board. If you can't take a doctor to sea, have a good first aid kit, with thorough instruction book, on board. Learn this stuff. Take courses; be ready.

Keep your systems for propulsion, fuel, cooking, and heating from catching on fire. Keep these systems tight, and keep them clean.

Put out a fire by smothering it to cut off its oxygen supply; by flooding it to cool it below the burning point; or by removing the combustible material. Turn off the juice to an electrical fire. Have tested and inspected fire exting-

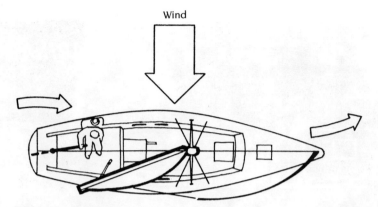

Boat should normally carry some weather helm, sails (in toto) trying to head her up, and rudder turned (tiller to weather) to keep her from heading up.

mainsail trimmed
mainsail eased

When rudder falls off, reef mainsail, so sails won't try to head her up. Steer by trimming mainsail in to head up, and easing it out to head off.

"When your rudder falls off, be able to steer with balanced sail combinations." (Normal steering, upper; using the mainsail as a rudder, lower.)

uishers at the ready. Ventilate any piece of machinery or equipment before lighting it off.

Think of alternate ways of steering your vessel if the primary way fails. Have an emergency tiller; have access to your steering gear; have spare parts.

When your rudder falls off, be able to steer with twin screws, with balanced sail combinations, with a jury sweep, or perhaps a combination of two or even all three such systems.

One night we were out in a twin-screw powerboat that

was an indifferent steerer, requiring all sorts of unexpected wheel turnings every other second. Finally the groaning steering gear gave up the ghost, but we found she handled about as well with the throttles as she had with her rudders and went gaily on about our business, even to backing her into her slip at the end of her run. Of course the time to try these shenanigans is some fine day when your steering gear is working perfectly.

When thinking about making distress signals, think in terms of what you yourself would respond to. Use the radio if you must; learn the discipline and procedure of using it correctly. Use flares or any other attention-getter.

Have other vessels on your mind, as well as your own. Watch for other vessels in trouble; when you see one, go to her assistance.

If you keep the sea for pleasure, give way in everything to the working waterman.

MAN OVERBOARD

Perhaps the most fearful thing about going to sea is the thought of losing someone overboard and not being able to recover him. Remember the old rule: one hand for yourself and one hand for the ship. Impress on people the desperate need to hang on. Don't let people go to dangerous places on the vessel in rough weather unless it is absolutely necessary. In such a case, change course to minimize the motion.

When running, watch the boom like a hawk. Be especially alert to the inadvertent jibe. Crashing booms can knock non-duckers overboard (and otherwise damage them).

Use the best harnesses you can buy or make. Everybody should have his own harness and be responsible for its maintenance. Lifelines should be both high and low, plenty strong, and big enough so you can get ahold of them.

"Lifelines should be both high and low, plenty strong, and big enough so you can get ahold of them."

The only effective life jacket is the one you're wearing when you fall overboard. Having wet suits or survival suits available in a hard chance makes sense. Have a strobe light and a whistle.

When sailing alone or standing watch alone, with self-steering gear keeping your vessel on course, tow a line with a buoy on the end of it so attached to the apparatus that a hard pull will override the steering gear and round the vessel up.

Have one or two life rings stowed aft on deck ready to be thrown. Attached to the life ring should be a ballasted, tall, stand-up buoy with a good-sized bright flag and a strobe

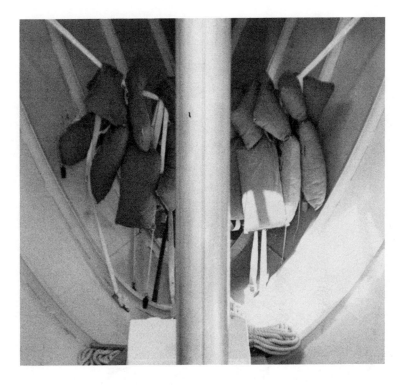

"The only effective life jacket is the one you're wearing when you fall overboard." Courtesy, Sail *magazine.*

light on it. Have 100 feet of bright-colored, floating polypropylene line between ring and buoy, so the whole business will give you a well-spread-out target to ease your vessel up to. In heavy weather, overhaul this rig often—like once a watch—to be sure it's all ready to go instantly without fouling anything. Nothing like overhauling a life ring to remind you to hang on.

If a person does get overboard, sing out "man overboard!" loud and clear to be sure everybody gets the word and jumps up on deck. Put your life ring and buoy in the water. Detail an *experienced* sailor, or two if you can spare them, to do absolutely nothing but keep their eyes glued

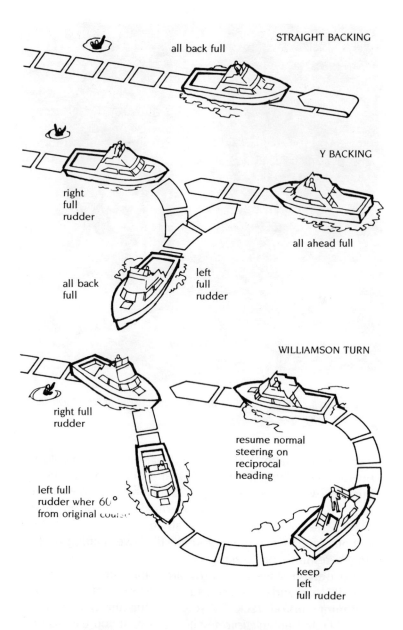

STRAIGHT BACKING

all back full

Y BACKING

right
full
rudder

all ahead full

all back
full

left
full
rudder

WILLIAMSON TURN

right full
rudder

resume normal
steering on
reciprocal
heading

left full
rudder when 60°
from original course

keep
left
full rudder

Picking up a man overboard when under power.

on the person in the water and point continuously at the person or at the point where they think the person is. It is absolutely vital that this lookout or these lookouts do not become disoriented or distracted by darkness, inter-vening seas, or the maneuvering and handling of the vessel. You may even want to do this vital job yourself, and leave it to others to bring the vessel to where you are pointing. A quickly thrown life ring with flagged and strobe-lighted buoy will, of course, help you keep track of the position of the man overboard.

When under power, the most basic maneuver for recovering a man overboard is to stop, then back up and retrieve him right over the stern. There's no quicker way to get him back on board. The trick is, though, to approach the man with considerable sternway, then kick ahead before you get to him, so you can then coast slowly back to him the last few yards with dead screws.

If sea conditions make backing straight down difficult or impossible, back her around in a quarter circle the way her stern naturally wants to go under the conditions, then kick ahead when perpendicular to your original course, contin-uing to turn the vessel in the same direction, and approach the man bows-on on the reciprocal of your original course. The track you have followed will resemble a cusp sticking out from your original track line. This is the fastest way to get back to the man bows-on.

In sharply reduced visibility, or if—perish the thought—there is a significant delay between the time when the man went overboard and the time when that fact became known on board, you must maneuver to retrace your steps. Under power, use the Williamson Turn to put your vessel back on her track heading the other way. Put the rudder over until the vessel has turned 60 degrees from her original heading, then shift the rudder and bring her all the way back around the other way until she is on the reciprocal of her original heading. This turn should put you close to your original track and going back along it. The turn may be made in either direction. If there's been a delay,

93

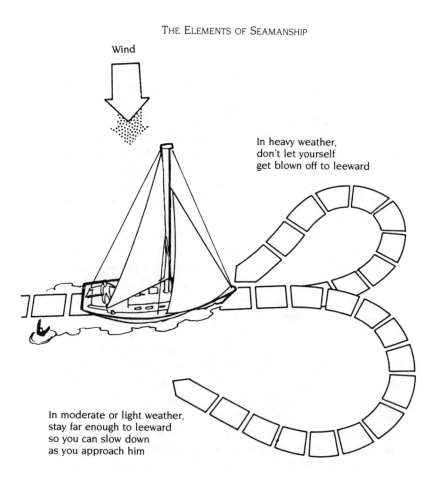

Wind

In heavy weather,
don't let yourself
get blown off to leeward

In moderate or light weather,
stay far enough to leeward
so you can slow down
as you approach him

"When turning back under sail for a person in the water, tack in heavy weather and jibe in moderate or light weather."

now it's time to figure probable time of the person's going overboard and adjust the course for set and drift and leeway. You'll need the coolest, calmest, most accurate dead reckoning track you can possibly get, lookouts who can really stare and listen, and a measure of good luck.

If under sail when a person goes overboard, with power available, use power and take in sail if you wish, but don't waste maneuvering time in making the change from sail to power. Start sailing the boat back to the person in the water even as you start the engine.

When turning back under sail for a person in the water, tack in heavy weather and jibe in moderate or light weather. Concentrate on not being blown off to leeward of the person in the water in heavy weather, and concentrate on being far enough to leeward of him in moderate or light weather so you can slow down as you approach him by letting sheets fly, luffing the vessel, or both.

Under either power or sail, approach the person in the water dead slow, bring him on the lee side (so you'll drift toward rather than away from him, and so you'll be pulling him over the low side rather than the high side), and get your vessel so close to him your heart is in your mouth for fear of running over him. Five feet away may be just out of reach.

When trying to recover a person from the water, there is nothing like a low-sided boat with a deep cockpit whose coaming is out near the rail. But rarely will you have such a secure place from which to reach far out and down over the side into the water. More likely, you'll be on a high-sided boat with wide decks. Now to reach the person in the water, you'll need to put a ladder over and climb down it, launch a life raft, rubber boat, or dinghy, or put one or more swimmers in the water. Obviously any person going over the side to rescue another ought to be dressed in the best flotation gear available and be tethered to the vessel, and any boat launched should also be tethered to the vessel.

LEADERSHIP

Leadership is vital on the water. If you are the captain, lead. If you are in the crew, follow. A vessel with more than one captain is in constant, unnecessary danger.

The captain is the one who must take full responsibility for the vessel and all in her. It is A Very Good Thing if he knows his stuff.

The captain must be considerate of his crew, keeping them from unnecessary danger and discomfort. One of my early mentors in seamanship told of cruising as a young man in a big schooner yacht under a famous skipper who had been down to Labrador and all that. One nice afternoon with the schooner sailing along on the wind with everything set, my mentor obligingly crawled to the end of the main gaff to clear the flag halyard. The famous captain forgot he had sent somebody aloft and tacked ship. It wasn't rough, so my mentor managed to hang on. Thus do reputations go up and down.

The captain is ultimately responsible for the water and food served the crew. Look well to your supplies of both. If everybody's worn out, heave-to for a good meal. Develop and keep your vessel's reputation as a good feeder.

Urge the crew to keep dry by putting on foul weather gear before spray or rain start to fly and by keeping it on a little longer than might be thought necessary.

Have everybody rest in good weather. Anytime you'll be underway more than 18 hours, set watches so that some of the crew can come on deck fresh. Everybody has his favorite watch system (mine for a long haul is standard Navy four-hour watches, but with no dogwatches, so you get the same watches every day and can really settle into a routine), but the choice of system is far less important than settling into some system.

Notice any bad habits brought on board your vessel by the crew and correct any that could be dangerous. Observe, for instance, just how somebody goes about slacking a line that is under heavy strain. See how early your helmsman realizes that the danger of collision may be deemed to exist. Never hesitate to interrupt sociality with essential ship's business; even great philosophical discussions must give way before the need to tack.

Have enough organization on board your vessel to run her smoothly. When being relieved on the helm, pass the course being steered, and talk about other vessels in sight, the vessel's position, navigational aids, the weather, and

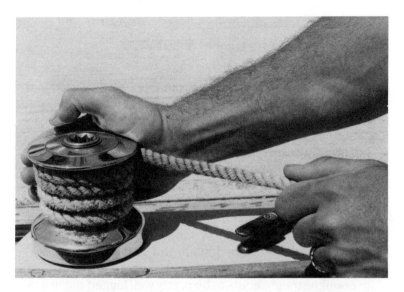

"Notice any bad habits brought on board your vessel by the crew and correct any that could be dangerous. Observe, for instance, just how somebody goes about slacking a line that is under heavy strain." (Above, right; Below, wrong.) Photos by Goben. Courtesy, Sail magazine.

anything out-of-the-ordinary about engine or sails. One of the nice things about being on the water is peacefulness; keep a reasonably quiet bridge or cockpit.

Ship's humor can be as funny as any ashore. Seagoing hilarity, however, often loses its edge when retold to those who were not on board the vessel when the laughter first rang out. Once, after long and busy fleet operations off Norfolk, Virginia, our destroyer was told to steam up Chesapeake Bay immediately and spend a whole night blasting the hell out of a low, sandy target island with five-inch projectiles. This we dutifully did, and when we turned around to head back out at six in the morning, we'd all put in enough straight hours to be pretty well fagged out. It was still my watch on the bridge, though, along with a third class quartermaster who came up to me and said, "Mister Taylor, how 'bout a raise?" Not terribly funny, but he said it just perfectly, I laughed hysterically, and I am still chuckling.

Clowning around has its place in a vessel, but never at the expense of seamanship.

One of the best things you can do to keep your reputation is to bring a vessel in from sea after a gale with a happy, reasonably well-rested crew and no damage to the vessel. Such success requires devotion to the vessel and devotion to the crew. If you're the master, watch over your vessel in hard weather. Keep exhaustion at bay, but remember Ben Franklin's (paraphrased) advice: "Up, sluggard; there'll be sleep enough in the harbor."

Keep a log on board your vessel. Writing down what went right and what went wrong helps you learn the elements of seamanship. Writing a log also lets you enjoy watery experiences a second time; reading a log prolongs the pleasure.

Study the history of seamanship and of vessels. Learn of the amazingly able seamen who have preceded us. Read the literature of the sea.

Spin yarns. Talk about the sea, its vessels, and its seamen. Discuss the elements of seamanship.

And now, here's wishing you a fair breeze and a following sea.

Appendix A

Sea State Table

Description and wave heights	Sea state
Calm glassy 0	0
Rippled 0 to 1 foot	1
Smooth 1 to 2 feet	2
Slight 2 to 4 feet	3
Moderate 4 to 8 feet	4
Rough 8 to 13 feet	5
Very rough 13 to 20 feet	6
High 20 to 30 feet	7
Very high 30 to 45 feet	8
Phenomenal over 45 feet	9

Beaufort Scale

Appendix B

Beaufort number or force	Wind speed (knots)	Description	Effects observed far from land	Effects on fishing smack	Effects observed on land
0	under 1	Calm	Sea like mirror.	Fishing smack becalmed.	Calm; smoke rises vertically.
1	1-3	Light air	Ripples with appearance of scales; no foam crests.	Fishing smack just has steerage way.	Smoke drift indicates wind direction; vanes do not move.
2	4-6	Light breeze	Small wavelets; crests of glassy appearance, not breaking.	Wind fills the sails of smacks which then travel at about 1-2 miles per hour.	Wind felt on face; leaves rustle; vanes begin to move.
3	7-10	Gentle breeze	Large wavelets; crests begin to break; scattered whitecaps.	Smacks begin to careen and travel about 3-4 miles per hour.	Leaves, small twigs in constant motion; light flags extended.
4	11-16	Moderate breeze	Small waves, becoming longer; numerous whitecaps.	Good working breeze, smacks carry all canvas with good list.	Dust, leaves, and loose paper raised up; small branches move.
5	17-21	Fresh breeze	Moderate waves, taking longer form; many whitecaps; some spray.	Smacks shorten sail.	Small trees in leaf begin to sway.
6	22-27	Strong breeze	Larger waves forming; whitecaps everywhere; more spray.	Smacks have doubled reef in mainsail; care required when fishing.	Larger branches of trees in motion; whistling heard in wires.
7	28-33	Moderate gale	Sea heaps up; white foam from breaking waves begins to be blown in streaks.	Smacks remain in harbor and those at sea lie-to.	Whole trees in motion; resistance felt in walking against wind.
8	34-40	Fresh gale	Moderately high waves of greater length; edges of crests begin to break into spindrift; foam is blown in well-marked streaks.	All smacks make for harbor, if near.	Twigs and small branches broken off trees; progress generally impeded.
9	41-47	Strong gale	High waves; sea begins to roll; dense streaks of foam; spray may reduce visibility.		Slight structural damage occurs; slate blown from roofs.
10	48-55	Whole gale	Very high waves with overhanging crests; sea takes white appearance as foam is blown in very dense streaks; rolling is heavy and visibility reduced.		Seldom experienced on land; trees broken or uprooted; considerable structural damage occurs.
11	56-63	Storm	Exceptionally high waves; sea covered with white foam patches; visibility still more reduced.		Very rarely experienced on land; usually accompanied by widespread damage.
12	64 and over	Hurricane	Air filled with foam; sea completely white with driving spray; visibility greatly reduced.		Very rarely experienced on land; usually accompanied by widespread damage.

*Based on scale from *American Practical Navigator* by Nathaniel Bowditch.

Wave Characteristics

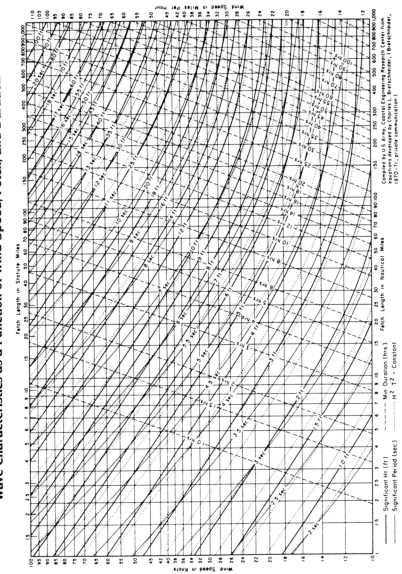

Wave Characteristics as a Function of Wind Speed, Fetch, and Duration

Index